"Bethany and Kristen have d[   ]   l 'true
north' in the pursuit of dating and love. If you've ever wanted a wise big
sister to help you navigate relationships, this book gives you two of them!
Their advice is practical, is grounded in truth, and will lead you to God's
heart for romance and sexuality."

—Dr. Juli Slattery, cofounder of Authentic Intimacy
and author of *Sex and the Single Girl*

"In *Love Defined*, Kristen and Bethany challenge the popular status quo
approach to relationships. Their ideas are radical. Countercultural. If
you're a young woman looking for true romance according to God's way,
you can't afford to miss this book!"

—Mary A. Kassian, author of *Girls Gone Wise*

"Kristen and Bethany are refreshing voices of truth and wisdom on the
subjects of love, dating, and sex. I am so glad to see these two sisters
coming together to present God's will for relationships. You'll devour
Love Defined, enjoy some great laughs, and most of all, define real, lasting
love for yourself. The truth is, we are not alone on this journey. God is
right here with us, unfolding His word and casting light as we put Him
at the center of our lives."

—Jennifer Strickland, founder of URMore.org; speaker;
author of *21 Myths (Even Good) Girls Believe about Sex*,
More Beautiful Than You Know, and *Beautiful Lies*

"I'm so impressed by the raw honesty, deep care, and biblical wisdom
found in this book. If you are looking for true love, don't continue without
this guide. If you've been burned by a relationship, this book will help
heal your wounds. Whether you are thirteen or thirty-one, this book is
full of wisdom for you. Listen to Kristen and Bethany as they plant you
beside streams of water to refresh you with God's true design for love."

—Sean Perron, director of operations at the Association of
Certified Biblical Counselors; author of *Letters to a Romantic:
On Dating* and *Letters to a Romantic: On Engagement*

"Today's dating culture thrives on hookups and heartbreaks, with young
women caught in a vicious cycle of hope-filled infatuation and crushing
disappointment. With marriage on the decline and the divorce rate on
the rise, it's pretty clear that modern dating methods are not working. I
believe God has a more glorious path for His girls, a way that is smarter

and leads to a stronger future. The practical and hope-filled truth found in *Love Defined* points women to a biblical approach to finding true love and establishing lasting relationships. I can't stress this enough—this book is a must-read for young women!"

—**Marian Jordan Ellis**, author of *Stand* and *Sex and the Single Christian Girl*

"The ancient wisdom of God's Word has never been more timely, and the seasoned wisdom of older women has never been more needed than in our sexually and relationally confused time. Praise God for Kristen's and Bethany's candor and grace in this readable, practical guide to romance and marriage. I pray countless Christian young women will be spurred on to obedience and godliness by these sisters' exhortation."

—**Candice Watters**, author of *Get Married*

"This is a book I want to give to every girl in my generation. In a culture that defines love in a hopelessly shallow and (ultimately) destructive way, Kristen and Bethany call us to a better definition. They point us to God's Word with uncompromising humility, honesty, grace, and transparency. This book will give you two new friends and faithful mentors. My prayer is that you will imitate Bethany and Kristen as they imitate Christ."

—**Jaquelle Crowe**, author of *This Changes Everything*

"Our concept of love needs a makeover. My friends Kristen and Bethany (founders of GirlDefined Ministries) are just the girls for the job. *Love Defined* is not just another book about romance. It's an invitation to see past the fairy tale and focus on something better. In a style that makes you feel like you're sipping coffee with a great friend, Kristen and Bethany invite you to look at love through the lens of the gospel. As they hold high the banner of true, lasting love, you will find your heart strengthened and your concept of love reimagined."

—**Erin Davis**, writer, blogger, and GirlDefined fan

LOVE
DEFINED

LOVE
defined

EMBRACING GOD'S VISION
FOR LASTING LOVE AND
SATISFYING RELATIONSHIPS

KRISTEN CLARK AND
BETHANY BAIRD

BakerBooks

a division of Baker Publishing Group
Grand Rapids, Michigan

Published by Baker Books
a division of Baker Publishing Group
PO Box 6287, Grand Rapids, MI 49516-6287
www.bakerbooks.com

Printed in the United States of America

Library of Congress Cataloging-in-Publication Data
Names: Clark, Kristen, 1987– author.
Title: Love defined : embracing God's vision for lasting love and satisfying
    relationships / Kristen Clark and Bethany Baird.
Description: Grand Rapids : Baker Publishing Group, 2018. | Includes
    bibliographical references.
Identifiers: LCCN 2017055473 | ISBN 9780801075568 (pbk.)
Subjects: LCSH: Single people—Religious life. | Christian women—Religious life. |
    Dating (Social customs)—Religious aspects—Christianity. | Marriage—Religious
    aspects—Christianity.
Classification: LCC BV4596.S5 C53 2018 | DDC 248.8/432—dc23
LC record available at https://lccn.loc.gov/2017055473

The names and details of some of the people and situations described in this book have been changed or presented in composite form in order to ensure the privacy of those with whom the authors have worked.

In keeping with biblical principles of creation stewardship, Baker Publishing Group advocates the responsible use of our natural resources. As a member of the Green Press Initiative, our company uses recycled paper when possible. The text paper of this book is composed in part of post-consumer waste.

18   19   20   21   22   23   24   8   7   6   5   4   3

To our amazing parents, Mike and Heidi.
Your investment in our lives has shaped us
into the women we are today.
We love you!—Kristen and Bethany

To my husband, Zack. Thank you for showing me
the beauty and power of Christ-centered love.—Kristen

Contents

Contents

PART ONE

Happily Ever Disaster

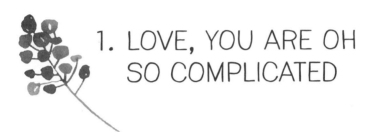

1. LOVE, YOU ARE OH SO COMPLICATED

The clock read 4:21 p.m. In exactly nine minutes, my life would change forever. This was the day I (Kristen) had dreamed of for twenty-four years. Standing in the bridal suite, I gently adjusted my floor-length veil and white wedding dress. Up until this point, the day had been a crazy blur. Last-minute venue prep. Steaming my wedding dress. Applying waterproof mascara. Trying to get my straight hair to stay curled. Oh, and helping a bridesmaid who ironed a hole in the front of her dress. The day was in fast motion. Every minute flashed past as quickly as I blinked.

Until now.

The bridesmaids were out of the room. The moms were being seated. My dad was waiting nervously right outside the bridal suite door. For the first time all day, the room was quiet. Everyone was gone except for one person . . . Bethany. This girl was my best friend. My maid of honor. My adventure partner for the past two decades. My sister.

Standing across from each other, we silently soaked in this moment as time stood still. And then, without warning, Bethany did the unthinkable. With my makeup finished and the touch-up powder out of reach, she burst into tears. And that's all it took for me. After I burst into tears myself, both of us stood there crying and laughing.

"I can't believe you're making me cry right before I walk down the aisle!" I said, laughing.

Scrambling for some tissues, she laughed through her tears and said, "Sorry . . . it all just hit me. I can't believe you're about to get married. Things will literally never be the same again."

"I know," I said, dabbing my cheeks. "It's crazy. I honestly thought this day would never come. And now here we are."

"No kidding," Bethany replied. "You're actually getting married . . . to an amazing guy. I guess that means there's hope for the rest of us single girls!" Putting her hand on my shoulder, Bethany smiled warmly and said, "Seriously, Kristen. I'm really excited for you. This is an incredible day. God is so good, and Zack is perfect for you."

Standing across from each other, we silently soaked in this moment as time stood still.

"Okay, don't make me cry again," I said, fanning my eyes.

This special moment, as we embraced in a long sister hug, was one neither of us would ever forget.

And with that, our dad knocked on the door and said, "Time to go, girls."

But First, Heartbreak

As beautiful and romantic as my wedding day was, my relationship journey wasn't always picture-perfect. Four-and-a-half years before Zack and I got married, I went through one of the hardest breakups of my life.

"Look, you're not supposed to know this, but Ryan's shopping for rings!" Bethany said to me in an excited whisper.

"What?" I asked with huge eyes. "Seriously? How—"

"I can't tell you any more," Bethany said. "Just make sure your nails are looking good over the next few weeks."

I was surprised by this news, but not shocked. Ryan and I had been seriously getting to know each other for six months. Deep in my heart, I truly believed he was the one. *So this is what true love feels like?*

My parents and siblings loved Ryan (well, most of my siblings). And even though we came from completely different types of families and backgrounds, we shared a lot of common interests. Even though our relationship had endured some rocky patches, we seemed to be pushing forward. He loved Jesus. I loved Jesus. We got along great. We enjoyed each other's company. What else did we need?

At twenty years old, I thought I was getting off easy in the love department. *How awesome would it be to get married now and avoid the drama of single life?* I thought. Confident I had found the one, I figured a little wedding research would be harmless. With my head in the clouds, I turned on my computer and searched for wedding dresses. Little did I know that exactly one week from this point I would be flying away on a plane with a shattered heart.

At twenty years old, I thought I was getting off easy in the love department.

The next few days turned out to be some of the hardest in my *entire* life. My dream world came crashing down before my eyes. Although my relationship with Ryan looked great on the outside, it was covered with red flags. He and I had convinced ourselves we were "perfect" for each other. But we weren't. Not in reality.

My infatuation with Ryan had blinded me to the many issues and problems in our relationship. And sadly, Ryan's rough past wasn't as much of his past as it was his present.

After a lengthy conversation with my parents, my fears were confirmed. Getting married to Ryan would be an extremely unwise decision. As this realization flooded my mind, I burst into tears.

I cried that entire night. I cried that entire next day. Bethany and I even cried together. It was painfully hard.

After Ryan and I broke up, I desperately wanted to get away for a little while. I needed time to think. To pray. To breathe. I hopped on a plane with Bethany to go visit our grandparents in Chicago. As the plane took off early the next morning, I honestly wondered if I would ever be able to love again.

He Loves Me, He Loves Me Not

One year after Kristen's breakup with Ryan, I (Bethany) met an amazing guy named Justin. I was falling hard for this guy. The chemistry was instant. He was funny, tall, good-looking, easygoing, and he loved Jesus. What more could a girl want?

Justin and I met through some mutual friends. His personality was everything I had ever imagined in a future husband. Our growing interest in each other was becoming obvious to everyone around us.

With my parents on board and excited about our relationship, Justin and I began getting to know each other more intentionally. As a nineteen-year-old girl, I couldn't believe how my life was panning out. I had always wanted to get married young. And with Justin being several years older, it seemed like the perfect love story. My head was in the clouds. My heart was on fire.

My head was in the clouds. My heart was on fire.

After several more months of getting to know Justin, I just knew. *He's the one. He's totally the one.* Up until this point in life, I had never been in a serious relationship. Crushes? Yes. Lots of them. But never a real relationship like this one. I had never met a guy like Justin. I had never been friends with a guy who I genuinely wanted to marry. Until now. Justin changed everything.

Over the next few weeks things continued ramping up. Justin began meeting with my dad for some good guy-to-guy chats. Even though Justin was a fairly new Christian, he was anxious to grow in his relationship with God. I loved his passion for theology. I loved his desire to know the Bible. He seemed perfect in every way. The fairy tale movies I had watched as a little girl were coming to life right before my eyes. *This love thing is so easy!*

And then—out of nowhere—my entire world came crashing down. "We need to talk."

Those were the four little words that popped up on my phone. I quickly clicked on Justin's text message. My heart started pounding. Something wasn't right. Our text messages were always surrounded by hearts and smiley faces. This text was plain. To the point. No fluff.

After texting back and forth for several minutes, my phone rang. It was Justin.

"I hate to do this by phone," he said with a sad tone, "but since I'll be gone on my business trip for the next week—" He paused. "Well, I . . . I just need to tell you what I'm really thinking."

The next thirty minutes were a shock and a blur. Justin told me that he really liked me but had come to realize "we" wouldn't work long-term. He explained that his interest in God wasn't as strong as it seemed. He confessed that he didn't genuinely share the same convictions as he had led me to believe. He told me his life would be going in a very different direction from this point on.

After what seemed like forever, this awful phone call finally ended. With my heart crushed and my dreams pulverized, I hung up the phone. I cried for the next three weeks. Love wasn't all that simple after all.

Love and Romance Are Complicated

If there's one thing the two of us have learned over the past decade, it's this: romantic relationships are complicated. Those charming little princess movies we watched as kids didn't do either of us any favors as we grew older. Our simplistic view of love and romance was quickly shocked into reality.

As teen girls, we faced new challenges regularly. *Is it okay to tell this guy I like him? How do I get this cute guy to notice me? Is dating around okay? Is it possible to be "just friends" with a guy? What if my best friend likes the same guy as I do? How do I guard my heart? What about flirting? Physical boundaries? Late-night phone calls?*

> *Our simplistic view of love and romance was quickly shocked into reality.*

We had a lot of questions. Our parents and others wisely helped us work through these issues. But it wasn't easy.

And then we grew a little older and everything changed. Again. *What qualities are important in a future husband? How do I set God-honoring boundaries? What are the nonnegotiables? How do I know if he's "the one"? What do red flags look like? How do I stay content when all my friends are getting married?*

Question after question. Situation after situation. Year after year.

Despite our childhood fantasies, we quickly learned that there wasn't a one-size-fits-all mold. Navigating romance and relationships wasn't as simple as Hollywood made it seem.

The fact that you're reading this book probably means you've experienced some complications too. We're guessing you've asked similar questions. Faced similar challenges. Experienced some form of heartache. Wrestled through singleness. Wondered if God's Word had anything to say.

Sister, you're not alone. We've been there. Others have been there. It's tough. Navigating the waters of love isn't a piece of cake. And it doesn't help that modern culture is feeding us conflicting messages about how to navigate best. The movies tell us to follow our hearts. Love songs tell us to find the one. And our friends give us all sorts of random advice.

A twenty-three-year-old single woman named Chelsey wrote to us expressing her struggle in this area. "It's so hard to know what's right anymore when it comes to romantic relationships! The culture around me is throwing its view on me every day, and I'm not even sure what to think anymore."

Can you relate? Whether you're eighteen or well past your thirties, you've probably experienced the confusion and complication associated with romantic love in some form or another. And if you haven't, you've probably experienced the longings and struggles of being single. If you're anything like the two of us, you've wondered if there's a better way. A wiser way. A God-honoring way.

In short, there is. There is a much better way. Thankfully, the Creator of the universe didn't leave us hanging when it comes to our love lives.

Why We Wrote This Book

Instead of offering you a new dating program or an ABC solution to finding the one, the two of us want to offer you a biblical approach for true love and lasting relationships. It's pretty clear that modern methods for pursuing romance and relationships aren't working. We need something better. Something smarter. Something lasting. The two of us are calling a time-out in the modern game of love and declaring "enough is enough." Hollywood, we're calling your bluff. Unless we, as Christian women, break free from our modern culture's broken view of love, we will continue to struggle down the same miserable path.

We need something better. Something smarter.

Over the past decade the two of us have opened God's Word and discovered a radically better approach to love and relationships—an approach that places Christ at the center of our love lives.

Despite your current season of life, we are confident that God's Word has specific and helpful answers for you. After all, God designed love and marriage, so He would know how to navigate it best.

Whether you're single and struggling to stay content, involved in a confusing relationship and need clarity, trying to guard your heart and stay pure, or wondering how to navigate the path to marriage successfully—*God's Word has answers.*

Regardless of why you picked up this book, we want you to know that the Bible has practical, applicable, and insightful wisdom for helping you navigate your love life—all for God's glory.

THROUGHOUT THE PAGES OF THIS BOOK YOU WILL DISCOVER

- A BIBLICAL APPROACH FOR TRUE LOVE AND LASTING RELATIONSHIPS;
- GOD'S SPECTACULAR DESIGN FOR LOVE, MARRIAGE, AND SEX;
- WHAT IT TAKES TO BUILD A STRONG FOUNDATION NOW FOR YOUR FUTURE MARRIAGE;
- PRACTICAL INSIGHTS FOR SUCCESSFULLY NAVIGATING THE PATH TO MARRIAGE;
- HOW TO LIVE A LIFE OF PURPOSE, INTENTION, AND SATISFACTION AS A SINGLE WOMAN;
- ESSENTIAL QUALITIES TO LOOK FOR IN A FUTURE HUSBAND;
- HOW TO BUILD A CHRIST-CENTERED LOVE STORY THAT LASTS, AND MUCH MORE.

The two of us aren't experts on the topic of love. We aren't relationship gurus or professional matchmakers (although we've had some success!). But we know the One who is. And as we've applied His truths to our lives, we've learned how to trust Christ more deeply and find our total satisfaction in Him. When Christ took center stage in our love lives, everything changed.

If you're tired of riding the waves of infatuation, crashing on the shores of heartache, and struggling down the road of confusion, join us on this new journey. A journey to discovering God's beautiful and incredible design for true love and lasting relationships.

Say hello to *love defined by God.*

CHAPTER 1
STUDY GUIDE

*"Regardless of your current season of life,
we are confident that God's Word has
specific and helpful answers for you."*

1. In what ways have you experienced "complications" when it comes to love and romance?

   _____

   _____

   _____

2. Which of the following questions have you asked yourself? Underline any that apply.

   Is it okay to tell this guy I like him?

   How do I get this cute guy to notice me?

   Is dating around okay?

   Is it possible to be just friends with guys?

   What if my best friend likes the same guy as I do?

   How do I guard my heart?

   What about flirting?

   Physical boundaries?

   Late-night phone calls?

   What qualities are important in a future husband?

   How do I set God-honoring boundaries?

   What are the nonnegotiables?

How do I know if he's "the one"?

What do red flags look like?

How do I stay content when all my friends are getting married?

3. What has been most influential in shaping your current view of love and romance (e.g., movies, music, novels, friends, parents, church, God's Word, etc.)?

_____

_____

_____

4. List three things you're hoping to learn by reading this book.

_____

_____

_____

MAKE IT *personal*

Let's start things off right. Take a moment to stop and pray. Ask God to help you have an open heart and mind as you seek to embrace His vision for lasting love and satisfying relationships.

2. SEEING THROUGH THE FAIRY TALE FACADE

I (Bethany) couldn't believe my eyes. Was that really Jacob Wood and Kaitlyn Martin walking into the conference building together? Holding hands? I grabbed my cell phone and immediately dialed up Kristen.

"Guess who I just saw walking into the conference?" I blurted into the phone.

"Ummm . . . I have absolutely no idea," Kristen said, confused.

"C'mon, think for a second!" I replied. "This is big! Like Prince Charles and Princess Diana big!"

Then Kristen knew exactly who I was talking about. "No. Way. You've got to be kidding me. Jacob and Kaitlyn? I thought they broke up years ago?"

"I guess history has a way of repeating itself," I said half joking. "Okay, gotta run. The opening session is about to start."

As I sat down in the auditorium, I couldn't help but stare at Jacob and Kaitlyn. They looked like the perfect pair. I didn't have to watch long to notice how completely infatuated they were with each other. The way he stroked her hair. The way she smiled at him. The way they looked into each other's eyes.

Over the next six months I watched Jacob and Kaitlyn fall head over heels for each other. Jacob treated Kaitlyn like a princess and won her heart quickly. Any conflicts that arose were quickly overshadowed by Jacob's smooth words and sweet kisses. He guaranteed Kaitlyn that she was his girl. He was done playing the field. He was done messing around. He was ready for real life. He was ready to focus on her.

At least that's what he said.

On a brisk October evening, under a starry night sky, Jacob got down on one knee and asked Kaitlyn to become his wife. With tears in her eyes and a heart full of innocent joy, she said, "I couldn't imagine marrying anyone else but you. *Yes!*"

Less than three months later this Hollywood-worthy couple tied the knot.

I wish their story ended there. I wish I could say they lived happily ever after. But they didn't. Little did anybody know how heartbreaking the next few years would be.

Before I share the end of their story, let's jump back in time to get some background on what led them to this point.

I grew up with Jacob and Kaitlyn. Although I wasn't best friends with them, we hung out here and there during high school. Kaitlyn was drop-dead gorgeous, naive, and a little new to her Christian faith. Jacob was smart, good with words, popular, and a little too handsome for his own good. Jacob was a ladies' man—and he knew it. All the girls knew it too. Well, all the girls except for Kaitlyn, that is.

I wish I could say they lived happily ever after.

Jacob and Kaitlyn dated for a few months during their sophomore year of high school. Jacob was completely enamored by Kaitlyn's gorgeous looks. Unfortunately, after the initial excitement wore off, his interest slowly wore off too. He was ready for something new. Something different. Something fresh.

Without giving it a second thought, Jacob texted Kaitlyn and said, "Hey, I need to move on. I just don't love you anymore."

The text totally caught Kaitlyn off guard. She was shocked and confused. She wondered what had gone wrong. Why had he dumped her?

Even though Jacob had ditched Kaitlyn abruptly, she never quite got over him. She missed him. She wanted him back. She wanted her hand to be in his. She wanted to feel the way she had felt when he had told people she was his girlfriend. It didn't matter to her that he had bounced from one girlfriend to the next after dating her. She desperately wanted him back.

After several years, Jacob became interested in Kaitlyn once again. Seeing his interest return made her heart run wild. All her old feelings went into full throttle. She assumed her intense passion for Jacob was a sign of true love. Hand in hand with Jacob once again, Kaitlyn felt like her life was a perfect fairy tale.

And this takes us back to where I started their story at the beginning of this chapter.

Let's pick up right after their wedding.

After Jacob and Kaitlyn got married, I honestly believed their relationship would work out. I naively assumed their good looks and intense passion would be enough to carry their marriage long-term. I assumed Jacob would transform into a mature, faithful, pure, and godly man. I thought Kaitlyn would instantly become a wise and mature Christian woman.

Unfortunately, marriage has a way of exposing sin, not erasing it.

Three years after Jacob and Kaitlyn got married, the unthinkable happened. I'll never forget the look on Kaitlyn's face as she walked into the restaurant where we were meeting.

"He left me," she muttered. With her mascara running down her face and tears overflowing into her hands, she said, "He left me . . . for another woman."

I couldn't believe my ears. I thought marriages were supposed to just work out. I thought young couples as popular and gorgeous as Jacob and Kaitlyn were somehow above disaster. I thought her good looks would keep a guy no matter what. I thought life would be great for them.

I thought her good looks would keep a guy no matter what.

It was through their tragic relationship that my eyes were opened to the devastating effects of an infatuation-based marriage. I quickly learned that it takes a lot more than good looks and passion to maintain long-term love. Unlike the movies, this fairy tale story didn't end with a "happily ever after." This was real life. And it was awful.

A Sad Realization

We wish Kaitlyn's story was a rare exception, but it's not. As the two of us entered our early twenties, we quickly realized that most modern relationships were not thriving. Heartache, pain, struggle, and divorce were quickly becoming common realities for those around us. Instead of watching our peers get married and live contented lives, we watched many of their marriages end in divorce.

It's no secret that we, as modern women, live in a relationally broken generation. With the divorce rate pushing the 50 percent mark,[1] many of us are experiencing this brokenness firsthand. Whether it's your own love life, your parents' marriage, or a friend's relationship, you've probably seen the devastation.

Recently, I (Kristen) had a conversation with a group of single girls. It seemed as though every one of them had experienced something difficult or painful regarding their own romantic relationships. One girl revealed the brokenness she had experienced when her boyfriend unexpectedly broke up with her to chase after a different girl. Another girl shared about the guilt she'd been feeling since losing her virginity to her ex-boyfriend. Another one told of the confusion she was facing as a result of dating a non-Christian coworker.

Despite the obvious heartache and dysfunction that we, as single women, experience, romantic relationships don't seem to be improving. In fact, it seems as though they are continuing to become more miserable, painful, and broken. Like a snowball growing bigger as it rolls down a hill, relational devastation seems to be growing bigger with each passing year.

The Fairy Tale Facade

When the two of us were in our late teens, we honestly believed relationships would just work themselves out. We never really stopped to consider what makes a relationship truly successful. We figured that if two people had sparks and chemistry when they got married, then the relationship would last. But watching Jacob and Kaitlyn's relationship crumble caused us to stop and question our perspectives. It made us reconsider our definition of true love and our idea of a lasting relationship.

In the weeks that followed Jacob and Kaitlyn's divorce, the two of us realized that we had been living with a false understanding of love. We naively assumed that somehow couples could thrive on infatuation, sparks, and chemistry for a lifetime. We had unintentionally believed that modern couples could define love according to their own terms and still have lasting results.

This false view of love is a direct result of what we call the Fairy Tale Facade.

The Fairy Tale Facade is like a beautiful false front. From the outside, it looks really good. Imagine a temporary front covering on the outside of an old, ugly building. The exterior looks great, but behind the false front is nothing more than a wreck.

The Fairy Tale Facade promotes the idea that we can completely ignore God's design for love, sex, and romance, and still have lasting, satisfying results. It's the idea that Hollywood can define love according to its own terms and still create happily ever afters. It's the false belief that we can ignore the Creator's perfect plan for our lives and still achieve complete satisfaction apart from His design. Despite all the lofty promises the Fairy Tale Facade offers, it's nothing more than a false front.

> The Fairy Tale Facade is like a beautiful false front. . . . The exterior looks great, but behind the false front is nothing more than a wreck.

Instead of blindly buying into the Fairy Tale Facade, we, as Christian women, need to stop and evaluate its results. We need to take a serious look at the status of modern relationships and see what's truly working and what's not. We need to open our eyes, ask good questions, and look at real statistics. We need to get behind the false front and acknowledge the rubble.

The Fairy Tale Facade can be exposed only if we're willing to be honest with the reality of modern relationships. We need to stop and ask some pointed questions.

If Hollywood's version of true love works so well in the movies, then why doesn't it work in real life? If adultery is portrayed as free of consequences in TV shows, then why is it incredibly painful in real life? If sex outside of marriage seems to bring such great satisfaction in chick flicks, then why does it leave us empty and needing more in real life? If one-night stands are so fun and thrilling, then why do they leave us so miserable? If lasting love is defined by two beautiful people falling in love, then why is divorce so rampant?

When we, as modern women, answer those questions honestly, we quickly realize the deception of the Fairy Tale Facade. We clearly see how unrealistic and shortsighted culture-defined love truly is:

BAD GUYS DON'T SIMPLY TURN GOOD WHEN THEY GET THE GIRL.
NAUGHTY GIRLS DON'T JUST TURN NICE WHEN THEY GET THE GUY.
ADULTERY ISN'T CUTE AND SWEET.
SEDUCTION DOESN'T BRING TRUST.
ONE-NIGHT STANDS AREN'T CONSEQUENCE FREE.
SEX OUTSIDE OF MARRIAGE COMES WITH BAGGAGE.
DIVORCE HAS LASTING CONSEQUENCES.
THE LIST GOES ON.

Despite the way Hollywood continually tries to convince us that true love can be found apart from God, the two of us aren't buying it. We've seen the Fairy Tale Facade leave too many women disillusioned and empty. We're done with the false front. We're done buying into its empty promises. We're done accepting the way it glamorizes sin. We're done sitting back while it tries to hijack God's design. We're calling it out for what it truly is. *False.*

Exposing Hollywood's Track Record

Without even realizing it, the two of us used to believe the lie that Hollywood had the solutions for lasting love and thriving relationships. From the outside, it appeared as though most actors and actresses had perfectly functional love lives. It seemed as if they had discovered the secret to true love that average people could not attain. The magazines often portrayed their lives in a perfect light.

However, when we dug below the surface, we discovered that this portrayal of perfection couldn't have been further from the truth. Some of the most famous actors and actresses had some of the most dysfunctional relationships. Their real lives were often the exact opposite of the happy characters they played in the movies. In light of this reality, we decided to do some in-depth research on a few of the most famous modern celebrities. Unfortunately, the research went quickly and the results were repetitive. Short marriages followed by quick divorces seemed to be the trend among the superstars we researched. In fact, we discovered that the marriages of elite celebrities in our society have an even higher divorce rate than the average person.[2] Despite these celebrities' wealth, beauty, and fame, lasting love seems harder for them to hold on to.

One website reported that "celebrity divorces are so prevalent that it's impossible to keep up unless you work for TMZ or spend all day reading about 'shocking splits' in gossip magazines. While the national divorce rate rests between 40 and 50 percent, celebrities seem to change their spouses almost as often as they change their sheets."[3]

Sadly, the celebrities we most idolize as relational "experts" often have the most broken track records. The *UK Daily Mail* came out with an article shedding light on this topic. "The famous may dazzle us with their $100,000 fairy story weddings, 15-tier cakes and horse-drawn carriages, but all too often these weddings are followed, in quick succession by a bitter and tortuous fallout and divorce played out in the public eye in grisly detail."[4]

As modern women, we often look to our favorite celebrity idols and wish we had their lives. We become mesmerized by the fame and glamour. But in reality, the fairy tale lives they appear to be living are nothing more than a facade. The glamour is nothing more than a false front. Beyond the red carpet, camera flashes, and

> *When we, as modern women, answer those questions honestly, we quickly realize the deception of the Fairy Tale Facade. We clearly see how unrealistic and shortsighted culture-defined love truly is.*

sparkly clothes, their lives are often a revolving door of hookups, breakups, and relational brokenness.

We must wake up to this reality and acknowledge that Hollywood doesn't have the answers to lasting relationships. Our celebrity idols aren't experiencing truly vibrant marriages. The methods they're using for finding and maintaining relationships aren't working.

The glamour is nothing more than a false front.

However, despite the lack of relational success in Hollywood, we, as Christian women, often embrace the exact same methods. Without questioning anything, we run down the same broken path. Why do we do this? Because Hollywood's method is the most popular one out there. It's the default method for modern relationships.

The two of us have decided to call this broken method the Merry-Go-Round Method for Modern Relationships. In the next chapter, we're going to explore exactly what this method is, and why it's leaving us on an endless cycle of heartache.

CHAPTER 2

STUDY GUIDE

The Fairy Tale Facade promotes the idea that we can completely ignore God's design for love, sex, and romance, and still have lasting, satisfying results.

1. In your own words, describe the Fairy Tale Facade.

_____

_____

_____

2. In what ways have you seen the Fairy Tale Facade negatively affect you or people you know?

_____

_____

_____

3. Put a check next to each statement you've seen play out in real life:

   ☐ Bad guys don't simply turn good when they get the girl.

   ☐ Naughty girls don't just turn nice when they get the guy.

   ☐ Adultery isn't cute and sweet.

   ☐ Seduction doesn't bring trust.

   ☐ One-night stands aren't consequence free.

☐ Sex outside of marriage comes with baggage.

☐ Divorce has lasting consequences.

4. Why do you think good looks and romantic passion aren't enough to sustain a relationship long-term?

_____

_____

_____

5. If Hollywood's version of true love works so well in the movies, then why doesn't it work in real life?

_____

_____

_____

MAKE IT *personal*

Search your heart and ask God to show you any lies you've believed about the Fairy Tale Facade. Finish each sentence below in your own words.

I'VE BELIEVED THE LIE THAT . . . _____

I'VE BELIEVED THE LIE THAT . . . _____

I'VE BELIEVED THE LIE THAT . . . _____

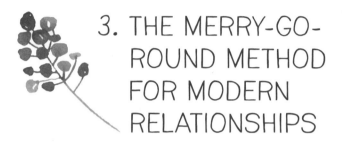

3. THE MERRY-GO-ROUND METHOD FOR MODERN RELATIONSHIPS

The bright lights and flashing signs of the theme park were a welcome sight to us and our excited group of friends. While I (Bethany) was busy dreaming about the big boat that swings through the water, Kristen was leading our little group toward her favorite ride, the Spinning Wheel. Within minutes Kristen spotted the ride and excitedly jumped in line to spin her brains out.

I stood against a nearby wall dreading the thought of getting on this ridiculous ride. *Who in their right mind would want to spend four solid minutes in a spinning torture chamber?* I thought to myself. The ride started and I soon heard the laughter and screams of Kristen and our friends.

After what seemed like a lifetime, the bell rang and the ride slowly came to a halt. I watched Kristen and our friends dizzily stumble toward me, panting for breath and laughing. Kristen grabbed my hand and started pulling me toward the line.

"You've got to try it," Kristen said, determined. "It's so much fun! And it doesn't even make you feel dizzy."

Why I said yes, I'll never know.

Bottom line: the Spinning Wheel was awful. I hated it from the first spin around to the very last. I felt sick for the rest of the day. I will never ever (even to this very day) get on a spinning ride again. I learned my lesson the hard way, and I'm not making that mistake again.

Never-Ending Spinning

When the two of us look at our culture's method for modern romance, we see a lot of parallels between it and the crazy spinning ride. From the outside, everything looks fun and exciting. The lights are bright, the laughter is loud, and the screams are abundant. Everyone (well, almost everyone) is spinning around, having the time of their life. And then the ride stops. The nauseated passengers stumble toward the exit wondering if the ride was worth it.

Our culture's method for relationships has a way of doing the exact same thing. Like the nauseated passengers who go around in circles, we, as modern single women, hop on board a similar relationship ride. We spin in repetitive circles and wonder why we reap nauseating results. We stumble out of one romance and into another, hoping for something more. But nothing changes. Confused and disoriented, we continue getting back in line for another crazy ride.

We stumble out of one romance and into another, hoping for something more.

Just like the Spinning Wheel, a merry-go-round is designed to turn in constant circles. The ride goes around and around, creating a similar spinning experience as the wheel.

If a rider doesn't like the merry-go-round experience, she should jump off. She should try a new ride that operates in a completely different way. Simply moving from a spinning amusement park ride to a playground merry-go-round won't change the experience. She's still spinning around. Same routine. Different seat.

Just like a merry-go-round and the Spinning Wheel, the Merry-Go-Round Method for Modern Relationships works the same way. It's a never-ending cycle of spinning.

This method is the most popular out there. It's the one Hollywood encourages. It's the one we hear idolized in popular music. It's the default method for most single people today. It's the method you are probably using right now, or will use in the future.

> *The primary goal of the Merry-Go-Round Method is rooted in and fueled by a desire to please self.*

The primary goal of the Merry-Go-Round Method is rooted in and fueled by a desire to please *self.* This method is motivated by personal happiness. It isn't driven by a desire to bring God glory but rather a desire to satisfy ourselves.

THE GOAL OF THE MERRY-GO-ROUND METHOD = PERSONAL HAPPINESS

When personal happiness becomes our greatest pursuit in a romantic relationship, all our decisions will be driven by that motivation. Our focus is on getting what we want when we want it rather than on glorifying God.

The Merry-Go-Round Method for Modern Relationships is built on a five-step process. It starts with step 1 (which we're about to dig into) and works its way to step 5. We, as modern women, often hop on this relationship merry-go-round in hopes of finding our happily-ever-after ending. We start the relationship ride by finding a good-looking dude. Then we chase after him until we catch his eye. After we've caught him, we begin coasting on infatuation and feelings. As the relationship progresses we count on our guy to satisfy all our needs. If at any point we find ourselves unhappy or dissatisfied, we just assume we have the wrong guy; we must be riding around with the wrong dude! Instead of hopping off the merry-go-round, we look at the available options and start the process all over again. Around and around we go.

We are going to unpack the five-step process of the Merry-Go-Round Method for Modern Relationships. We're going to explore how it works in real life. As you read through the steps, see if you can relate to any of them. Have you ever unknowingly followed this method and ended up on the crazy merry-go-round?

Let's jump into step 1.

STEP 1: CATCH THE RIGHT GUY.

Girlfriend, it's time to start hunting. The perfect guy is out there. You just need to catch him. Get out of your comfort zone and get on the hunt. Do whatever it takes to catch the dude who will satisfy you. If you can find your soul mate, he will complete you and make you perfectly happy. He will be your Prince Charming. Your knight in shining armor. Your happiness maker. He will be everything you've ever dreamed of. You just need to focus on catching his eye and capturing his heart.

According to modern culture, this is the first step toward a lasting romantic relationship. *You must first catch the right guy.* Until you catch your man, you won't be truly happy. You need to keep your eyes open at all times. Just think. He could be the barista at your favorite coffee shop. He could be the waiter who serves you dinner at a local restaurant. He could be the new trainer at your gym. He could even be the guy jogging in your neighborhood who just happens to wave as you drive by. He could be anywhere. You must keep your eyes open.

Back in high school, I (Kristen) worked so hard to catch who I thought was the right guy for me. I was sure that if I could catch him, I would be totally satisfied. I believed he was the missing piece to my puzzle. I thought I needed him to be happy. I worked ridiculously hard to catch that guy's eye. Like a natural pro, I pulled out all the stops. To my delight, my moves worked. He noticed me. This guy and I eventually exchanged phone numbers, and I was feeling like *the woman*. I soaked up the attention he gave me and thrived knowing I was on his mind. Life felt wonderful . . . at least for that moment.

> *I believed he was the missing piece to my puzzle.*

If you've caught the right guy on the merry-go-round, you're ready for step 2.

STEP 2: COAST ON INFATUATION.

You're standing in line at your local bakery when the unimaginable happens. The cute guy behind the counter smiles at you in a way that says, "Hey, baby, I'm your dreamboat!" Your knees weaken and your mouth goes dry. It's obvious that you've just experienced love at first sight. Without hesitation, you mentally start planning your wedding with this bakery hot rod.

This is the next step toward your happily ever after: let your emotions run wild. Obviously the chemistry between you and this guy is a clear indication that you're meant to be. It doesn't matter that he's twenty years older than you. It doesn't matter that he's working part-time hours and still living in his parents' basement. It doesn't matter that he's using all his free time to play video games. None of that matters. The only thing that matters is the chemistry between the two of you. Right here. Right now.

You just need to coast on that infatuation. It will take you to your destiny. It will lead to your soul mate. Oh, and make sure you ignore the wisdom and advice of those around you. They aren't *you*. They don't understand the chemistry and sparks happening in your heart. Ignore any cautions or red flags they might bring up. Infatuation must be your compass for navigating your heart.

Despite how silly some of this may sound, it's what modern culture encourages single women to do. We are encouraged to make important romantic decisions while dazed by infatuation. Wisdom and discernment are nonfactors when it comes to the life-altering decision of marriage.

The emotions are strong. The chemistry is cranked up. Everything seems perfect in the moment. "The way many researchers describe this brain state [infatuation] overall is an 'idealization' of the one you love. You focus on the strengths (many of which might be imaginary) and are blind to weaknesses (many of which are readily apparent to outside observers). You 'idealize' this person to make them the kind of person you want them to be. It should be clear that if you're in this state you're in no position to make an objective choice if you rely on your feelings."[1]

This blinding state of infatuation is exactly what we see playing out in modern romantic relationships.

This blinding state of infatuation is exactly what we see playing out in modern romantic relationships.

I (Bethany) was infatuated with a guy in high school. I was crazily obsessed with him. I was convinced that anyone who offered me counsel was simply out of touch with reality. I didn't want my parents' advice. I didn't want Kristen's advice. I didn't even care if the wisdom offered to me was true. I was head over heels for this guy and wanted everyone else to enthusiastically like him too.

Hindsight is always 20/20, right? Of course, I can now clearly see how blinded I was by my infatuation for this guy. I had built him up to be a modern-day William Wallace. Nothing could change my perspective. I was sold on him.

Although it's estimated that infatuation typically lasts between twelve and eighteen months,[2] I definitely outdid the average with this guy. My infatuation really didn't begin to subside until the two-year mark. After two years, I finally began to see this guy with a clear head. I began to see him for who he truly was, not who I had imagined him to be.

Coasting on infatuation is a crucial step in the Merry-Go-Round Method.

Once you've hunted down your man and coasted on infatuation, you're ready for step 3.

STEP 3: CONCENTRATE ON YOUR FEELINGS.

Now that infatuation has set in, it's time to *concentrate on your feelings*. At this stage in the relationship, your feelings will be your best source of truth. If you feel good about the relationship, continue moving forward. You can determine if you're in love with your man simply by how you *feel* about him.

When it comes to the Merry-Go-Round Method, concentrating on your feelings is a must-have step. According to modern culture, your feelings will be the deciding factor for who you should or shouldn't be with. If it feels right, just do it. That's your motto and your guide. This motto is everywhere, so you should count on it to work for you.

I (Kristen) read an article that interviewed a famous country singer about one of his past divorces. The country singer said that he knew his previous marriage was over when his feelings began to transfer to a different woman. His feelings were his guide. And they were indicating to him that a different woman was his new soul mate. There was no talk of commitment, faithfulness, or self-restraint. The article made it clear that his heart was speaking and he needed to follow it. So, with a quick stroke of a pen, he signed the divorce papers and moved on to a new woman.

This is the world that we, as modern women, live in. We're told feelings are the defining and guiding factors that should lead us. We're told to "follow your heart" and "do what feels right." Our feelings are the road map for our love lives. If we follow them, they will lead us to our destiny.

Personal feelings are king when it comes to love and romance.

Toward the end of my senior year in high school, I (Kristen) met a cute guy and quickly progressed to step 3 in the Merry-Go-Round Method. This guy and I had serious chemistry. Despite the obvious problematic differences between the two of us, I was concentrating on my feelings, and they were telling me this relationship was right. I liked him. He liked me. We were meant to be.

In step three of the Merry-Go-Round Method, there is no voice of wisdom or reason. Personal feelings are king when it comes to love and romance. Any concerns, red flags, or outside wisdom should be discarded if your feelings confirm your direction.

Once you've hunted down your man, coasted on infatuation, and concentrated on your feelings, you will be ready for step 4.

STEP 4: COUNT ON HIM TO SATISFY YOU.

You've finally found your dream man. This guy *has* to be your soul mate. He is the one destined to satisfy all your needs. He's your Prince Charming. He should make you feel like a queen—at all times. Your job is simply to count on him to satisfy you. Go ahead and place all your hopes, expectations, and desires onto his shoulders. If he's your true love, he will make you happy at all times.

According to step 4 in the Merry-Go-Round Method of Modern Relationships, a guy's entire purpose is to make his girl's life better. He exists to bring her happiness. To make her feel secure. To meet all her needs. To read her mind and to know what she wants without her having to tell him. It's his entire job to satisfy her—and he better do it well.

When it comes to modern relationships, single women are taught to view guys as their happiness-makers. We don't even realize it, but this step is engrained into our brains. *He better make me happy. He better satisfy me. He better know when to bring me flowers and chocolate (dark chocolate, that is). He better know how to cheer me up when I'm frustrated. He better be the most thoughtful man at all times.*

A friend of ours named Kendra recently shared about how she had thoroughly applied step 4 to her relationship. On her and her boyfriend's first Valentine's Day as a couple, Kendra had high expectations. She wanted him to go above and beyond and treat her like royalty. She wanted roses and special gifts. She wanted constant doting. She wanted him to anticipate her every desire and satisfy them with precision.

Just imagine her reaction when the day didn't go according to her perfect plan. She was devastated. It didn't matter that her boyfriend had tried his best to make the day meaningful and special. Kendra's expectations had been shattered. She did what any devastated woman would do in a situation like that . . . she threw a big-girl tantrum. She let him know how sad, disappointed, and frustrated she was. He was supposed to be her happiness-maker, not her expectation-dasher.

Once you fully embrace step 4, you will be at the pro level on the Merry-Go-Round Method. At this point you are ready to move on to step 5.

STEP 5: CRY WHEN IT FAILS (THEN GO BACK TO THE BEGINNING AND DO IT ALL AGAIN).

If at any point in the Merry-Go-Round Method you stop feeling in love with your guy, call it quits. If your infatuation wears off, end it. If your feelings change, look for romance somewhere else. If he doesn't satisfy your every need and meet all your expectations, say goodbye. End the relationship the moment he stops making you completely happy. Apparently he wasn't your soul mate after all. It will be painful, so go ahead and cry as much as you need to.

Sadly, this final step is almost always inevitable.

However, according to our culture, there is still a bit of good news at this point in the process. Once you've cried enough tears and recovered from your heartbreak, just go back to step 1 again. Simply start the process over. Start hunting for a new man (because the guy you were with obviously wasn't the right one). It's time to hop back on the Merry-Go-Round Method and start working through the steps once again.

STEP 1: CATCH THE RIGHT GUY.
STEP 2: COAST ON INFATUATION.
STEP 3: CONCENTRATE ON YOUR FEELINGS.
STEP 4: COUNT ON HIM TO SATISFY YOU.
STEP 5: CRY WHEN IT FAILS.

Maybe this time around, or the one after that, you will actually find your true love. Just keep circling around because it may take five, six, or even seven times until you find your "perfect match." And even if the relationship does result in marriage, the Merry-Go-Round Method will be there for you if things don't work out. So start preparing now for a lifelong, nauseating ride on the merry-go-round.

The Method That Rules the Relationship World

So there you have it—the five-step method that rules the modern relationship world. If you keep an eye out for the Merry-Go-Round

Method, you'll notice it everywhere. It's in pop music. It's in popular movies. It's in reality TV shows. It's on social media. It's the foundation for your friends' relationships. Since this method permeates almost everything in modern culture, many of us have adopted it by default.

Looking back on some of our earlier relationships, we (Bethany and Kristen) unknowingly embraced certain aspects of the Merry-Go-Round Method. The culture had impacted our thinking more than we had realized. As expected, the Merry-Go-Round Method didn't serve us well. It didn't help us find the satisfaction we longed for. It didn't help us keep Christ at the center of our romances.

The Merry-Go-Round Method is an "all about me" method.

The reason this method produces such bad results is because it's primarily rooted in one thing: self-centeredness. The Merry-Go-Round Method is an "all about me" method. My happiness. My fulfillment. My satisfaction. My pleasure. My rules. My way.

Until we, as modern women, intentionally choose a Christ-centered approach, we will continue spinning in never-ending, nauseating circles.

Jumping Off the Merry-Go-Round

When we realized how broken the Merry-Go-Round Method was, we knew something had to change. We didn't like the results it was producing in our lives. We didn't like how self-focused and self-absorbed our romantic pursuits had become.

Instead of continuing to ride the merry-go-round, we realized that we could choose something better. We could approach relationships in a completely different way. As we studied what God's Word had to say about love, we realized the Merry-Go-Round Method isn't built on a biblical foundation. It's nothing more than a cheap imitation of God's good plan. So, without looking back, we decided to jump off the merry-go-round (we'll unpack more about God-defined love in the chapters to come).

As the two of us have strived to embrace God's design for true love and romance, we have been able to navigate relationships in a much more God-honoring way. The more our hearts have changed from being self-focused to Christ-focused, the more content and satisfied we have become. We hope you will take a leap of faith and join us on this journey to discovering God's vision for true love and lasting relationships.

CHAPTER 3

STUDY GUIDE

"Until we, as modern women, intentionally choose a Christ-centered approach, we will continue spinning in never-ending, nauseating circles."

1. Why is the modern method for relationships similar to a merry-go-round?

   _____

   _____

   _____

2. Fill in the blank: the goal of the Merry-Go-Round Method=

   _____

   What are some of the biggest problems you see with this goal?

   _____

   _____

   _____

3. Write out each of the five steps below.

   Step 1 _____

   Step 2 _____

   Step 3 _____

   Step 4 _____

   Step 5 _____

   Which of the five steps stands out to you the most? Why?

4. How have you seen the negative effects of the Merry-Go-Round Method play out in your life or the life of someone you know?

_____

_____

_____

5. In what ways does your current view of relationships need to change from being self-focused to more Christ-focused?

_____

_____

_____

MAKE IT *personal*

Will you join us in jumping off the self-focused merry-go-round? If so, take a few minutes to write out a personal prayer asking God to help you develop a more Christ-centered approach to love and relationships.

PART TWO

Bringing Back
True Love

4. FROM LITTLE-GIRL CRUSHES TO BIG-GIRL RELATIONSHIPS

By the time we hit our early twenties, we had each experienced heart-wrenching breakups. Remember Ryan and Justin? Yep. Those guys. Our fairy tale dreams weren't exactly panning out. *Ummmm . . . Cupid? Did you have a slight misfire?* Real life wasn't turning out the way either of us had always imagined. Instead of being married to our Prince Charmings by age twenty-one, we both found ourselves painfully single.

As our dreams melted away before our eyes, our trust in God was put to the test. We had no idea what the future held. We were both faced with the challenge to surrender our love lives to God.

Looking back now, we both can clearly see how God used those breakups to do some serious renovation in our hearts. He used the heartache and pain to drive us to His truth. The two of us had no idea how profoundly God would use our breakups with Ryan and Justin as launching pads for our own spiritual growth.

The next few years would prove to be crucial in our journey to understanding God-defined love.

Now that you understand what the Merry-Go-Round Method looks like, see if you can spot some of the pitfalls in our individual relationship journeys. Like most girls, our journeys with love and romance started with butterflies and crushes at the local neighborhood playground.

Boy in Jean Shorts

I (Bethany) clearly remember my first crush. I was nine years old when we met. Well, we actually never officially met. Now that I think about it, I don't even know his real name. Anyway, he was always hanging out at the playground my mom took me and my younger siblings to. He was such a heartthrob! My heart would flutter every time I saw him. But the thing that really caught my eye? His shorts. Yep. You read that right. He wore the same pair of denim shorts every. single. day. And I adored it. After several weeks, Kristen and I gave him the genius nickname, *Boy in Jean Shorts*. I know, I know. Really smart.

Since I was too scared to talk to Boy in Jean Shorts, I would sneakily stalk him on the playground, spying on him from the top of the jungle gym and secretly watching him on the swings. As a nine-year-old girl, I was already knee-deep in infatuation. I didn't know a lot about love at this point, but I knew this much—I liked this boy. Without being taught by anyone, my God-given, natural desire for romantic love was already budding.

Sparkly Haired Dude

While Bethany was swooning over Boy in Jean Shorts, I (Kristen) was developing a more refined crush. Being a year and a half older, I was hitting double digits with my age. I was in the big leagues now. No more playground crushes for me. I had advanced to crushing on my older brother's friends. My latest crush was three years older than I was and played on my brother Michael's baseball team.

Watching this cute boy run around the baseball field gave me butterflies. And the thing that really caught my eye? Nope, not his shorts. It was his hair. Not only did he have amazing hair, he did something extra special to it. Instead of using plain old hair gel like all the other boys, my crush took it to the next level. He would put little silver sparkles inside his gel bottle to create a sparkly effect. When he doused his dark head with that special hair gel . . . ooooh, baby, watch out! His hair actually sparkled as he ran around those bases. I was in love.

Since appointing secret nicknames runs in my family, I gave him the endearing nickname *Sparkly*. I was totally and completely infatuated by him.

As a young (but very tall) ten-and-a-half-year-old girl, I was already forming my own ideas about love. Without being formally taught by anyone, I started to believe true love was based primarily on feelings.

And with that, the merry-go-round started turning in my heart.

Without being formally taught by anyone, I started to believe true love was based primarily on feelings.

Hello High School

As the two of us grew older, our little-girl crushes slowly turned into big-girl crushes. Our early high school years brought with them a whole new set of questions and challenges. The magnetic pull and desire for love was still there but was now intensified. Instead of spying on boys from the playground or watching baseball players run around the field, we were actually talking to guys face-to-face.

Guys began noticing us and striking up conversations. They offered us attention in new and exhilarating ways. We quickly learned the art of "subtle" flirting (the Christian girl's way) and milked the attention for all it was worth.

Even though we were both homeschooled, our city had a huge homeschool program with opportunities to participate in competitive sports. During our high school years, we both played varsity basketball, so we spent a lot of time at the courts. Guess who else spent a lot of time at the courts? Really tall, good-looking basketball dudes. Since the two of us are really tall (6'1"), we had a special eye for those tall guys. Between the two of us, our older brother, and our younger siblings, we spent a lot of time at various gyms watching games and practices. As a result, both of us met a lot of cute guys that way too.

I (Bethany) distinctly remember sitting in the stands during one of my sibling's games, just staring down at my crush. He was sitting six rows in front of me but didn't realize I was behind him. I wanted him to notice me, so I did what any innocent Christian girl would do—I threw my shoe at him. Okay, okay. I didn't throw it directly at him, but I threw it right next to him. Of course, like the gentleman he was, he picked it up and turned around to see where it came from. And there I was, acting innocently shocked that my shoe had "fallen off."

I (Kristen) wasn't much better. Shortly after I got my driver's license, Bethany and I were heading home after one of our local basketball tournaments. As we passed by some restaurants, I recognized one of the cars in the parking lot.

"That's Derek's car!" I screamed out. I was crazy about this Derek guy. We had talked only a few times, but I could tell he liked me. Like a wannabe NASCAR driver, I did a screeching U-turn in the middle of the road, barely slowing down, and zoomed into the restaurant parking lot.

"Okay," I said to Bethany while catching my breath, "let's just walk inside casually, see where he's sitting, and then sit somewhere nearby. We won't say anything. We'll just see if he notices me."

"Okaaaay," Bethany said, smirking.

And with that, we nonchalantly walked inside. Derek noticed me right away. His friends started laughing and teasing him. After a few minutes his friends walked over and handed me a paper with Derek's phone number written on it. That was that. I was too shy to call him, so nothing else happened. Mission accomplished. I guess.

Getting More Serious

As the two of us entered our later high school years, things started getting more serious. Instead of throwing shoes at guys and doing NASCAR moves, bigger things started happening.

I (Kristen) had a random guy chase me down and try to kiss me during a church youth group event. Bethany had a guy friend try to convince her to make out with him "just for fun." A total stranger left a love note on my car windshield inviting me on a date. Guys handed both of us heartfelt love letters, invited us to dances and parties, and asked us out on dates.

For the first time, we were forced to stop and evaluate our personal boundaries and standards. What did we want our love lives to look like? What did God's Word have to say about all this?

For the first time, we were forced to stop and evaluate our personal boundaries and standards.

Thankfully our parents saw these things happening and called a time-out. Since the two of us are the oldest of the five girls in our family, our parents knew they needed to help us establish boundaries. Quickly. Since we had a great relationship with our parents and genuinely wanted to honor God in our lives, we were open to hearing their wisdom and input.

The two of us, along with our parents, sat down and had some incredible heart-to-heart conversations. We talked about dating, relationships, purity, communication, and boundaries. We had a lot of questions, and our parents were excited to work through them with us.

As our parents taught us more about God's plan for romance, love, sexual intimacy, and marriage, our eyes were opened to bigger truths. The two of us loved what we were learning and wanted to know more. Both being avid readers, we went to our local Christian bookstore and purchased a bunch of recommended books on the topics of love, dating, and marriage.

After devouring these books, we each saw more clearly God's purpose for love and romance. We still had a lot to learn, but we were making progress. We started realizing the pitfalls of the casual dating scene. We began to understand the dangers of shortsighted romantic relationships. We were confronted with questions, such as "Why get involved in a romantic relationship if you're too young to even consider marriage?" Or "Why would you date someone you could never see yourself marrying?" And "If you build your relationship on feelings, what happens when the feelings are gone?"

We wanted to be intentional with our love lives.

Question after question flooded our minds. As we sought God's Word for answers, we could see the wisdom in what our parents, and these books, were telling us. Then and there, in our later high school years, we made the personal decision to stay out of the casual dating scene. We saw the wisdom in waiting until we were a bit older to engage in romantic relationships. We wanted to be intentional with our love lives. We wanted to honor God with our purity. We didn't want to get into a relationship unless it had the potential to be something more.

After Ryan and Justin

Since both of us had chosen to avoid the casual dating scene, we didn't enter serious relationships until after high school. And that's when Ryan and Justin hit the scene. Each of those relationships was marked by intentionality and purpose. We willingly involved our parents in the process because we wanted their input and wisdom. The physical boundaries we had set in place also helped the two of us embrace purity.

Even though we were striving to honor God in these relationships, we still didn't have all the puzzle pieces in place. Without realizing it, we were buying into two of the lies of the Merry-Go-Round Method: *concentrate on your feelings* and *count on him to satisfy you.*

Unknowingly, Bethany had placed a lot of expectations on Justin, and Kristen had done the same to Ryan. We each looked to our respective guy to fully satisfy us. To meet all our needs. To make us feel secure and happy all the time. Slowly but surely, our eyes shifted away from Christ and onto these guys. As a result, our breakups were just that much more devastating to each of us.

It wasn't until we both fully recovered from those breakups that our eyes were opened to just how much we still had to learn. The two of us jumped back into God's Word and saw more clearly where we had gone wrong.

We discovered that *who* we marry is just as important as *why* we marry. We learned that Christ has to remain at the center of our relationships in order to build a foundation of genuine Christlike love. We learned that God didn't create marriage just for our happiness; He created it ultimately to bring Him glory.

These truths were huge, and they were rocking our worlds. We'll unpack these truths in the chapters to come.

Bethany's Journey

The months and years that followed my relationship with Justin were some of the best spiritual growth spurts of my life. God

57

opened my eyes to areas of selfishness and pride in my own heart. I realized how out of place my priorities had been. I saw clearly how Justin had become an idol in my heart.

God was not only opening my eyes to my own sin but also expanding my view of romance and marriage.

*We discovered that **who** we marry is just as important as **why** we marry.*

I specifically remember listening to a message about biblical relationships that radically changed my perspective. I don't even remember who the Bible teacher was, but he shared truths that profoundly reshaped my mind-set.

In a nutshell, here's what I learned.

Instead of just looking for a nice Christian guy to marry, I need to be more intentional. Just because a guy is a Christian doesn't automatically mean he is a good fit for me (or that I am a good fit for him). Good marriages are built on more than two nice Christians getting married. Since the purpose of marriage is to glorify God and serve Him well *together,* I realized that I need to marry a guy with whom I could serve the Lord effectively.

That new perspective changed the way I evaluated "options." It changed the way I prayed about a future husband. Instead of just looking at a guy's character, I looked at his vision. I looked at his passions. I looked at his driving purpose in life.

Where is this guy going in life? Does he have a kingdom mind-set? Do we share similar passions for life? Could I support his vision as his wife and teammate? Would we make a better team together than apart?

These new ideas blew my mind and greatly expanded my view of marriage.

As my perspective continued to grow and mature, Kristen was learning similar things as well. However, her path took a little bit of a different turn than mine. In God's providence, she just so happened to stumble on a certain young gentleman named Zack Clark.

Kristen's Journey

Like He did for Bethany, God was doing some serious renovation in my heart as well. I also began to understand more fully what true, Christ-centered love was. I began praying for my future husband in deeper, more specific ways. I learned how valuable wise counsel and godly input were to my romantic relationships. I also realized that feelings make terrible guides for relationships.

I am so grateful God opened my eyes to these truths when He did, because it prepared me immensely for what was about to happen. Little did I know that I would soon meet my future husband.

I still remember the first time I laid eyes on Zack Clark. I was at a Christian conference near Dallas. Zack was sitting ten rows in front of me and all I could see was the back of his head. I noticed him though. He was tall and athletically built, and he had sandy blond hair. I was instantly intrigued.

Little did I know that I would soon meet my future husband.

Throughout the conference our eyes met a dozen times. His tan complexion complemented his handsome face. I was seriously struggling to stay focused on the conference speakers.

We finally met on the evening of the last day. I was hanging out outside with some friends when he walked straight up to me and introduced himself. He was smooth and charming. We chatted for a few minutes, then quickly discovered that we both lived in San Antonio. My heart literally did a backflip. *He lives in San Antonio?!* I wanted to scream with excitement. As we parted ways that evening, I could hardly contain the flutters inside.

As exciting as that night was, I was about to get a really good lesson in patience.

To my dismay, nothing serious happened between Zack and me for several years. Yep. *Years.* We were friends, yes, and I could tell he was interested in me, but that was it. Nothing more. As year three rolled around, I seriously wondered if anything would ever happen between us. Let's just say God taught me a lot about trust and surrender during those few years. And you know what? That is exactly what I needed most. God was showing me I didn't need a guy in my life to be satisfied, but I could be fully satisfied in my relationship with Christ. I was learning that singleness wasn't a season to trudge through but a time of opportunity to glorify God in unique and productive ways.

Even though those years were hard for me, they were beneficial. Our casual friendship gave both of us the opportunity to get to know each other in a nonromantic way. We were able to see each other in normal, everyday situations and observe how we each interacted with others.

The more I learned about Zack, the more I could see our lives, visions, personalities, and passions aligning. His godly character became even more attractive to me than his looks. He was respectful, kind, genuine, and a total gentleman. He loved God and others, and I could clearly see that.

I just wasn't sure what *he* was thinking.

Then one warm September day, everything changed. Zack called me. With my heart melting, we chatted casually for a few minutes. Then he took the conversation to a deeper level. He shared that he had wanted to pursue a relationship with me earlier but had been advised to wait until he had completed college. He explained that the waiting had been extremely hard for him. I could totally relate.

Then, like a true gentleman, he sweetly explained that he didn't want to mess around with my heart. He desired to honor God and me. He expressed that he wanted to get to know me with the intention of seeing if he and I would be a good fit for marriage. This was such a relief to me. I never had to wonder where his priorities were. I always knew.

Zack and I entered into a purposeful relationship. Over the next ten months, I grew to deeply love this amazing guy.

I'll unpack more of the details of our relationship in the chapters to come. But for now, let me just say this: pursuing romance with Christ at the center of the relationship made such a difference for Zack and me. Surrounding ourselves with godly input and accountability was key as well. Understanding God's beautiful design for love, romance, and marriage enabled us to navigate our relationship with clarity like never before.

Where We Are Today

As we look back on our journey from little-girl crushes to big-girl relationships, we can't help but smile. God has done so much work in our hearts and lives, and we are grateful! As a result of looking to the Bible for truth, we've learned how to better navigate our love lives for God's glory. Our journeys aren't over though. Even today, God continues to convict our hearts and open our eyes to His truths in deeper ways. And it's exciting.

God wants to teach you powerful truths from His Word.

As you read this book, you are on a journey too. God wants to teach you powerful truths from His Word. He wants to take you from little-girl crushes to a mature, Christ-centered heart and life. He wants to broaden your view of love and relationships. He wants to show you how to honor Him well in your love life.

CHAPTER 4
STUDY GUIDE

*"God wants to take you from
little-girl crushes to a mature,
Christ-centered heart and life."*

1. Do you remember your first crush? What attracted you to him?

_____

_____

_____

_____

2. How have your perspectives on love and romance changed
   since the days of your first crush?

_____

_____

_____

_____

3. What was one thing that stood out to you about Bethany's
   relationship journey?

_____

_____

_____

_____

4. What was one thing that stood out to you about Kristen's relationship journey?

_____

_____

_____

_____

MAKE IT *personal*

Of all the married couples you currently know, which ones do you admire the most and why? Pick one of those couples and mail them a handwritten letter thanking them for the example that they've been to you.

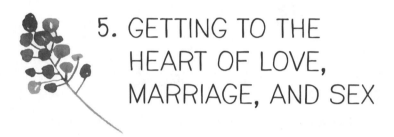

5. GETTING TO THE HEART OF LOVE, MARRIAGE, AND SEX

One spectacular love story took place many, many years ago. In fact, it was the very first love story ever. God Himself created the perfect match.

It's easy to read the story of Adam and Eve in Genesis and blow right past it. But if we pause for just a second, we will quickly see how incredibly romantic it truly is.

Imagine with us how this scene might have gone down. Adam is the only human on the entire planet (see Gen. 2:7). He's never seen another human. After tirelessly naming every animal, something dawns on him. Every animal has a perfect match, but he has no one (see Gen. 2:20). As Adam watches the last pair of animals trot away, his bachelor status becomes painfully obvious. An intense longing for companionship washes over him as he watches the busy scene around him. Everywhere he looks, he sees perfectly complementary pairs. Every animal has a mate. He has no one. As this reality floods his mind, he feels a deep desire for a mate.

He desperately wants to share his life with someone. But who? Scanning the busy scene once more, he wonders if he will ever find his perfect match.

With the sun moving slowly across the sky, something is about to change. The Creator of the universe has a plan. The most romantic love story of all time is about to unfold.

God sees. God knows.

After putting Adam into a deep sleep, God handcrafts the most beautiful and stunning creature of all. Taking one of Adam's own ribs out of his body, God intricately forms the last and final piece of His creation.

Adam rubs his sleepy eyes awake, and then he freezes. His eyes lock onto this new, breathtaking creature standing before him. Her soft and lovely eyes stare back into his. Realizing who she is, Adam's face explodes with joy. Jumping up from the ground, he excitedly exclaims, "This at last is bone of my bones and flesh of my flesh; she shall be called Woman, because she was taken out of Man" (Gen. 2:23). Embracing his bride in a tender hug, Adam closes his eyes and smiles. *God had a plan all along.*

The most romantic love story of all time is about to unfold.

Passionate Love Was God's Idea

The first love story. Handcrafted by God himself. This beautiful and true story of Adam and Eve proves that God is not only a good matchmaker but also a true romantic at heart. God Himself came up with the spectacular invention of marriage and sex (see Gen. 2:24–25; Eph. 5:31). These are beautiful gifts straight from His hands.

However, despite God's jaw-dropping track record, we, as Christian women, don't often view God as being the expert on these topics. We don't look to His Word for answers to our questions. Instead of viewing God as our starting place for wisdom on love and romance, we drift into believing He is some sort of romantic killjoy.

But in reality, that couldn't be further from the truth.

> *God's perfect Word contains more wisdom than every chick flick and romance novel combined.*

Instead of looking to popular magazines for advice, we need to look to the Author Himself. God's perfect Word contains more wisdom than every chick flick and romance novel combined. By submitting ourselves to God, we will learn how to build Christ-centered, God-glorifying relationships and marriages.

Despite what you've experienced, observed, or learned in the past about love, marriage, and sex, we encourage you to be open as you read this chapter.

Before we dive into God's spectacular design, take a moment to pray the following prayer.

Dear God,

Thank You for creating me and giving me Your perfect Word. I confess that I don't always look to Your Word as my source for truth and wisdom regarding love, marriage, and sex. Please forgive me. Please give me a heart of humility now to embrace Your truth in my life. Open my eyes to see any lies that I believe, and help me reject them. Thank You for being the God of redemption and forgiveness. Help me embrace Your truth from this point forward.

Amen.

Love Defined by God

I (Kristen) heard the story of a couple who had been married for over seventy years. As they entered their early nineties, the wife began to lose her sight. By the time her ninety-third birthday rolled around, she was completely blind.

Knowing how scary and hard this was for his wife, the husband stayed by her side every hour. He gently talked with her, prayed with her, sang her songs, cooked her meals, and combed her brittle hair. Wrapping his wrinkled hands around hers, he would softly whisper, "I love you more than life itself." Unable to look back at him, she would smile and say, "And I love you even more than that."

Day after day. Week after week. Month after month. He stayed by her side. He served her. He loved her. His unselfish love was fueled by his deeper understanding of God's faithful love to him. Having experienced God's sacrificial love for him for over ninety years, this older gentleman was compelled to love his wife in the same way.

One day the man's grandson was visiting and asked, "Grandpa, don't you get tired of just sitting with Grandma all day?"

Staring off into the distance, the grandpa paused for a moment then slowly said, "Son, she's been faithfully by my side for the past seventy years, showing me the sacrificial love of Christ. Now it's my turn to be faithfully by hers."

True love. That's it. Right there.

As modern women, we've been influenced by our society to define love quite differently. We think of love as being an emotional feeling, a magical spark, or a chemistry attraction. But, as we saw with the steps on the Merry-Go-Round Method, this is a shallow understanding of love.

Instead of basing our love on what the other person does for us, we need to learn the art of sacrificial love, as the older gentleman did. Instead of basing our love on something as unstable as our feelings and emotions, we need a firm foundation of true, biblical love.

If we want better for our love lives, our relationships have to be built on the unshakable foundation of love defined by God.

Looking to the Author of Love

This sweet old couple knew the secret of lasting love. That's why their marriage thrived for seventy-plus years. If you want a husband who will faithfully hold your hand during your most frail years of life, you need to marry a man who understands that kind of sacrificial, Christ-centered love. And if you want to faithfully serve and love your husband until his dying breath, you need to understand how to give that kind of love too.

To truly understand what God-defined love is, we need to look to the Author of love Himself. The Bible says, "God is love" (1 John 4:8). Since God is literally the definition of love, we can learn how to love by looking at His character and actions.

According to Romans 5:8, "God demonstrates his own love for us in this: While we were still sinners, Christ died for us" (NIV). Jesus, the King of the universe, sacrificed His life so we could have eternal life. Jesus gave up the glorious perfections of heaven to die a criminal's death on our behalf. That, right there, is true love. God-defined love is built not on a foundation of self but rather on a foundation of self-sacrifice.

God-defined love is built not on a foundation of self but rather on a foundation of self-sacrifice.

"The world takes us to a silver screen on which flickering images of passion and romance play, and as we watch, the world says, 'This is love.' God takes us to the foot of a tree on which a naked and bloodied man hangs and says, *This* is love."[1]

Jesus put His love on display through His sacrificial actions. True love is an action, not an emotional feeling. The most commonly used word for love in the Bible is the Greek word *agape*. It's used 259 times and essentially means "self-sacrifice."

As Timothy Keller says so well, "In sharp contrast with our culture, the Bible teaches that the essence of marriage is a sacrificial commitment to the good of the other. That means that love is more fundamentally action than emotion."[2]

For instance, I (Kristen) can tell Zack that I love him until I'm blue in the face, but until I put my love into action, it won't be believable.

Agape love is the foundation for Christ-honoring, lasting relationships.

Living Out True Love

Let's get really practical for a moment. It's a lot easier to "know" what agape love is, and a lot harder to actually live it out. How can we, as women, know if our relationships are marked by sacrificial love? What does agape love look like in everyday life? Thankfully, the Bible gives us some practical help.

The list below is a great tool to help you measure whether your romantic relationships are built on the right kind of love.

GOD-DEFINED LOVE IS . . .

HONORABLE (SEE 1 PET. 2:17)

KIND (SEE 1 COR. 13:4)

PURE (SEE PHIL. 4:8)

SELF-CONTROLLED (SEE 1 THESS. 4:4-5)

PATIENT (SEE GAL. 6:9)

OTHERS FOCUSED (SEE JOHN 15:12)

LONGSIGHTED (SEE HEB. 12:1-2)

FAITHFUL (SEE PROV. 3:3-4)

RESTRAINED (SEE 1 THESS. 4:3)

God-defined love is beautiful, strong, compelling, faithful, and powerful. Agape love is the polar opposite of what our sinful hearts are naturally inclined to give. But through the power of Christ, we have the strength to love others in this way.

Marriage Defined by God

Growing up in a family with eight kids has been a fun and crazy adventure for the two of us. We've loved it! Our siblings are some of our best friends. As wonderful as our siblings are, our family wouldn't be what it is if it weren't for two people: our mom and dad. Their faithfulness and commitment to each other, and to God, is what has made our family strong. With thirty-five years of marriage under their belt, our parents have shown us what lasting love looks like. They have given us the rare gift of having a front-row seat to a God-defined marriage. Even in their mistakes, they've modeled forgiveness and sacrificial love to each other.

> With thirty-five years of marriage under their belt, our parents have shown us what lasting love looks like.

As grateful as we are for our parents' marriage, we know that's not the norm in today's society. Many people today aren't growing up with parents who've modeled God-defined love to each other. With marriages falling apart (or couples never marrying at all), many modern women have never seen a biblical marriage in action. Marriage has been a picture of dysfunction, not beauty.

Without godly examples on display, we, as modern women, are struggling to know how to build solid marriages for ourselves. Our definition of marriage is being patched together from personal experience and/or the culture's broken examples.

To build Christ-centered marriages, we have to dig deeper into God's original plan and purpose for marriage.

The First Wedding

Without a fancy venue, a wedding dress, or an expensive cake, the first wedding took place. Adam and Eve's wedding was about as organic as they come. Surrounded by animals, colorful flowers, and the open sky, Adam took Eve to be his wife. God Himself handed Eve to her new husband (see Gen. 2:22). Without hesitation, the groom received his bride with great joy. God blessed the newly married couple and gave them a commission by saying, "Be fruitful and multiply and fill the earth and subdue it, and have dominion over the fish of the sea and over the birds of the heavens and over every living thing that moves on the earth" (Gen. 1:28). And with that, the first marriage was brought into existence.

Marriage. A magnificent institution created by God Himself. Understanding *what* marriage is needs to be our starting place. John Piper helps us understand this better. "In the beginning God created male and female with the purpose that they would marry and the two would become one flesh. So the Lord made woman from the side of man and then Adam says in Genesis 2:23, 'This at last is bone of my bones and flesh of my flesh; she shall be called Woman, because she was taken out of Man.' And here's this absolutely key verse that both Jesus and Paul quote: 'Therefore a man shall leave his father and his mother and hold fast to his wife, and they shall become one flesh' (Gen. 2:24). That verse is cited by Jesus and Paul as decisive in the meaning of marriage today."[3]

> *Marriage.*
> *A magnificent*
> *institution created*
> *by God Himself.*

God gave us Genesis 1 and 2 so we could see what true marriage is made of. One male. One female. For life. That is God's good and holy plan for marriage. Once we understand *what* marriage is, the next step is understanding *why* God created marriage. He could have created anything he wanted . . . but he chose one man and one woman to represent this holy union.

Understanding the why changes everything.

Why Marriage?

When God brought Adam and Eve together, he had a spectacular plan in mind. A plan much bigger than marriage itself. Since God is all-knowing, he planned the union of marriage with the future in mind. God knew Adam and Eve were going to sin. God knew humanity would be corrupted. God knew the world would need a Savior. In God's omniscient power, He created marriage to tell an incredible story. A story about Himself.

I (Kristen) have a beautiful hand-painted picture of a mountainous scene hanging in my house. Every time I look at this picture, I long for the fresh mountain air of Colorado (my second favorite state after Texas). This beautiful picture is a magnificent representation of the mountains I love. It reflects a beautiful scene. However, as much as I love this picture, it's only a representation of the real thing.

God created marriage to work exactly the same way.

Marriage, as lovely as it is, is only a picture of something *greater*. It's an earthly representation of something much grander. God placed the institution of marriage on the wall of this world as a representation of the gospel.

> THEREFORE A MAN SHALL LEAVE HIS FATHER AND MOTHER AND HOLD FAST TO HIS WIFE, AND THE TWO SHALL BECOME ONE FLESH. THIS MYSTERY IS PROFOUND, AND I AM SAYING THAT IT REFERS TO CHRIST AND THE CHURCH. (EPH. 5:31-32)

God's greatest purpose for creating marriage is to show the world an earthly representation of what Christ's covenant relationship looks like with His Church. Christ is the groom and the Church is His bride. As Timothy Keller says in his book *The Meaning of Marriage*, "This is one of God's great purposes in marriage: to picture the relationship between Christ and His redeemed people forever!"[4]

As Ephesians 5 shows us, the husband's role is to reflect a picture of Christ Himself and the wife's role is to reflect a picture of the Church. Christ (our heavenly groom) came to this earth, pursued His bride (the Church), sacrificed His life for her, made a lasting covenant with her (a promise that cannot be broken), and gave her a new name (child of God). Just as Christ loved, pursued, and sacrificed for His bride, husbands are called to do the same for their brides.

In marriage, the man is called to love his wife selflessly. To lead her in wisdom. To sacrifice himself for her good. "For the husband is the head of the wife even as Christ is the head of the church. . . . Husbands, love your wives, as Christ loved the church and gave himself up for her" (Eph. 5:23, 25).

On the flip side, the woman is called to respond to her husband's leadership as the Church responds to Christ. The woman is called to faithfully respect her husband. To welcome his leadership in their home. To partner with him in the work of the kingdom. "Now as the church submits to Christ, so also wives should submit in everything to their husbands. . . . Let the wife see that she respects her husband" (Eph. 5:24, 33).

Understanding marriage through a gospel lens is essential for us as Christian women. When a man and a woman live out their unique gender roles within the marriage covenant, they put the glory of the gospel on display as God intended. We show our lost and broken world a picture of Christ and His love for His bride (the Church) that would not be displayed otherwise. As Christian women, our primary purpose for getting married should be to glorify God. "As Christians, we don't believe that a happy marriage is the primary goal of life. Glorifying God is."[5] As women, we will glorify God most when we understand and live out His unique role for us as women/wives. We'll unpack more of what our beautiful and unique role is in the next chapter.

Scripture also reveals some other amazing purposes for marriage.

- COMPANIONSHIP (SEE GEN. 2:18)
- SEXUAL INTIMACY (SEE GEN. 2:24)
- HAVING A LIFELONG TEAMMATE (SEE PROV. 2:17)
- PRODUCING CHILDREN (SEE GEN. 1:28)

Marriage is a spectacular union created by God Himself. Desiring to get married for God's glory is a wonderful and biblical desire. "He who finds a wife finds a good thing and obtains favor from the LORD" (Prov. 18:22).

Approaching marriage with a selfless heart and gospel lens is the key to building a beautiful, Christ-exalting relationship.

Sex Defined by God

God created sex; it is *His* brilliant invention. Just like He created love and marriage, He is also the Author of sexual intimacy. It's not dirty. It's not inappropriate. It's not sinful. It's a spectacular design created by God to be enjoyed by husbands and wives within marriage (see Gen. 2:24; Heb. 13:4). As Dr. Albert Mohler says, "Sexual pleasure is not an accident of human biology—it is one of the Creator's sweetest gifts to human beings."[6]

*God created sex; it is **His** brilliant invention.*

Even though sex is part of God's good design, it often stirs up a wide range of feelings among Christian women. Some are negative. Some are positive. Some are in-between. Depending on how you were raised, the things you've experienced, and the choices you've made, your perspective on sex has most likely been influenced to lean one of two ways:

1. YOU VIEW SEX AS DIRTY, SHAMEFUL, AND AWKWARD AND ARE NOT EXACTLY LOOKING FORWARD TO IT IN MARRIAGE.
2. YOU VIEW SEX AS AN AWESOME AND POSITIVE THING THAT SHOULD BE EXPERIENCED RIGHT NOW WITHOUT ANY BOUND- ARIES OR RESERVE.

Each of these views leans in the opposite direction of the other, but both are wrong. Instead of leaning too far in one direction or the other, we need to get back to the center. We need to embrace a balanced, positive, and biblical perspective about sex.

Regardless of what you're feeling about this topic right now, we encourage you to allow God to work in your heart as you read this chapter. Ask Him to help you reject any lies you've believed, and instead embrace His truth regarding this area of your life.

An important foundational truth that we, as single women, need to understand is this: God created each one of us to be a sexual being. We don't magically transform into sexual beings once we get married. We are sexual beings from the moment we're born. Despite how you may feel at times, your sexual design isn't a curse; it's a beautiful part of God's good plan. Your desire for intimacy actually points to something much deeper. "Underneath your sexuality is the drive and desire to be known and loved. God created you as a sexual being so that you might understand what it means to long, to desire, and to crave intimate oneness. You have longings to share your heart, soul, and body with another person because God made you a deeply relational and spiritual woman. Your greatest need for intimacy however is to know the God who created you."[7]

The more you understand God's spectacular design for sex, the more equipped you will be to glorify Him in this area. Just as a flower thrives within the right context (good soil, lots of sunlight, and adequate rain), the gift of sex will thrive best (as God intended) within its proper context.

God gave us the entire book of Song of Solomon to show us the beauty of passionate and pure marital sex. As Timothy Keller puts it, "The book of Song of Solomon does much barefaced rejoicing in the delights of sexual love in marriage."[8] Many Bible scholars believe Song of Solomon is the actual love story between Solomon and his first wife (the Shulamite maiden). This beautiful love poem begins with the "courtship" phase of the relationship, where the couple expresses and reciprocates their love for each other (see 1:2–3:5). Then their love story moves into the wedding stage, where the bride and groom cleave to one another and share their first night of sexual passion together (see 3:6–5:1). And then, finally, the end of the poem paints a vivid picture of their marriage, showing the realities of a couple working through conflict, restoration, and growing in grace together (see 5:2–8:14). Song of Solomon is a candid and beautiful love story that should prepare us and get us excited about God's design for sexual passion within marriage.

> *Despite how you may feel at times, your sexual design isn't a curse; it's a beautiful part of God's good plan.*

The book vividly shows us that God specifically and intentionally created the gift of sex to be enjoyed only within the context of marriage (see Song of Sol. 4:1–16). God did not give the gift of sex to be enjoyed by single people (see Mark 10:6–8). Why? Because just as the marriage union points to the gospel, so does sexual intimacy. As intimate as the physical act of sex is, it's only a "picture" of the cherished covenant relationship that Christ has with His Church. Sexual intimacy is the *most* intimate act that we, as humans, have, and yet it's only a picture of how deeply God loves us.

As author Jennifer Strickland explains, "*Yada* is the Hebrew word for 'knew,' as in 'Adam knew his wife Eve' and she conceived and bore a son (Gen. 4:1). *Yada* means he knew her fully; he respected her deeply; he connected with her emotionally. Yada means she was fully known. Yada is the reason sex is best in marriage because it has to do with deep respect and emotional knowing—the kind of lasting love God has for you. So if sex is yada, there is nothing casual about sex."[9]

God intentionally created the act of sex to be powerful and bonding in marriage. It's like a magnet constantly pulling husband and wife toward each other. "Sex is perhaps the most powerful God-created way to help give your entire self to another human being. Sex is God's appointed way for two people to reciprocally say to one another, 'I belong completely, permanently, and exclusively to you.'"[10] This intimate act of knowing another human sexually creates a deep physical, emotional, and spiritual bond. Within marriage, this deep bond is a beautiful thing. When a husband and wife selflessly enjoy sexual intimacy within a covenant marriage, they will become even more unified. In this context, sex is pure, holy, unifying, and shame free.

However, outside of marriage, sex often has the opposite effect. It creates a false sense of love fueled by a perpetual longing for something more. "Sex outside of marriage eventually works backwards, making you *less* able to commit and trust another person."[11] It will never produce the blessings God intended it to have. It can't. Sex outside of marriage is not holy and beautiful but sinful and distorted (see Heb. 13:4). No relationship (no matter how passionate it may appear) can thrive as God intended while it is in opposition to the biblical design. It's essential that we, as Christian women, understand that God's plan for abstinence is truly for our own good. "The Bible does not counsel sexual abstinence before marriage because it has such a low view of sex but because it has such a lofty one. The biblical view implies that sex outside of marriage is not just morally wrong but also personally harmful."[12] The boundaries God has given to unmarried people are given out of a heart of love

> God intentionally created the act of sex to be powerful and bonding in marriage.

because He cares for us. Instead of buying into the lies or freely indulging in our desires, we must choose to take God at His Word. We must trust that our Creator knows what's best for us. We must believe His ways truly are for our good. His plan and context for sex are better than anything our sinful hearts desire.

Here are just a few of the incredible blessings and benefits of sex within marriage:

- PASSIONATE SEXUAL PLEASURE
- POWERFUL MARITAL ONENESS
- CHILDREN BORN INTO YOUR FAMILY
- PURE AND COVENANTAL BONDING
- INTIMATELY KNOWING YOUR SPOUSE

In all of this, though, we must remember an extremely important truth: sex isn't the answer to our happiness. Sex isn't the ultimate prize for getting married. As a single woman, be careful to steer clear of the lie that future sexual intimacy will meet all your needs. It won't. It can't. As incredible as sexual intimacy is, our greatest need is not for sex but for spiritual intimacy with our Savior. Whether a woman is single or married, her greatest needs will only be met when she's faithfully walking in a relationship with Christ. And that can happen right now. "We must remind [ourselves] that sex simply cannot fill the cosmic need for closure that our souls seek in romance. Only meeting Christ face-to-face will fill the emptiness in our hearts."[13] The more you build an intimate relationship with Christ right now, the more fulfilled you will become.

The two of us know that the topic of sex can often stir up unwanted memories, regrets, and painful emotions. This can be hard and feel almost crippling at times. It can be tempting to allow your past choices and circumstances to define your identity. But as a daughter of Christ, you must remember that your identity is not determined by what you have done or what has been done to you. Your worth and value as a woman does not hinge on your past, present, or future choices or circumstances. You are loved by God and valuable to Him as His precious creation.

Nothing we can do will ever separate us from His love and forgiveness. "For I am sure that neither death nor life, nor angels nor rulers, nor things present nor things to come, nor powers, nor height nor depth, nor anything else in all creation, will be able to separate us from the love of God in Christ Jesus our Lord" (Rom. 8:38–39). However, the love of God should compel us to repent of our sins and seek His forgiveness. The Bible says that if we humble ourselves and seek God's forgiveness, He will grant it to us. According to 1 John 1:9, "If we confess our sins, he is faithful and just to forgive us our sins and to cleanse us from all unrighteousness."

> *You are loved by God and valuable to Him as His precious creation.*

God can cleanse your past. God can redeem your future. Although sin may have some lasting consequences, you can walk in freedom from this point forward. We encourage you to take a moment to read appendix A (Finding Freedom and Forgiveness from Past Sexual Sin) on page 243. We've written in more detail about how you can find freedom and forgiveness from past sexual sin.

A PERSONAL WORD from *Bethany*

As I write these words, I am still single. I've never had sex. In fact, I've never even kissed a guy (saving it for the wedding day). Girl, I get it. Waiting is hard! But by God's strength in my life, I've been able to save sex for my future husband. As much as I long for a husband to enjoy these awesome gifts with, I'm choosing to trust God's good plan. Instead of wallowing in my singleness,

I'm focusing on pursuing a vibrant and fulfilling relationship with Christ.

As excited as I am to experience sexual intimacy some day, I know it's not the answer to my happiness. To keep sex in its rightful place in my life, I have to constantly remind myself that Christ is the only One who can truly satisfy me. The more I work on my relationship with Him (through Bible reading, prayer, worship, etc.), the less of a desperate longing I feel for other things. I've also noticed how helpful it is for me when I'm actively involved in my Christian community. Being plugged in to Bible studies and church has helped me surround myself with other like-minded singles. This type of regular fellowship encourages me to stay on the right path.

I truly don't know if God has marriage in store for my future. But if He does, I want to experience sex for the first time with my husband. Although the culture looks at me like I'm crazy, I'm putting my confidence in God's Word. I want to challenge you, as a single woman, to join me on this exciting journey of purity and faithfulness. Regardless of your past, today can be the day you choose to walk a God-honoring path for His glory.

A PERSONAL WORD from Kristen

When I got married to Zack, we were both virgins. With nervous excitement and anticipation, we approached our wedding night with great joy. We were newbies. Total amateurs. The culture told us that "practicing" before marriage was essential, but we decided to follow God's plan instead. And you know what? Our honeymoon was a pure, beautiful, and passionate adventure! We enjoyed God's gift of sex for the first time together. It wasn't embarrassing or scary, but I'll be honest—I was extremely nervous! As amateurs, we had a lot to learn, but that's what made it so special. And although it may feel awkward and scary at first, that's okay—because you have your entire lives to learn and grow together.

I didn't realize this at the time, but our commitment to God's plan *before* marriage acted as fuel for staying committed to God's plan *after* marriage. Our faithfulness to God and to each other built a strong foundation of trust and unity in our marriage. I have no regrets about doing things God's way. And neither does Zack. Was it hard to wait? Yes! Did it require a lot of patience and self-control? Yes! (I'll unpack more of my love story with Zack later in the book.) But God's grace was sufficient, just as He promises in His Word. "My grace is sufficient for you, for my power is made perfect in weakness" (2 Cor. 12:9).

As a married woman, I want to challenge and encourage you to stay the course. Don't give up. Don't grow weary. Don't take your eyes off Christ. Look to God for your strength, and He will help you walk in purity both physically and emotionally from this point forward.

Embracing God's Spectacular Design

God's spectacular design for love, marriage, and sex is the missing link that modern culture doesn't have. Instead, the culture is promoting counterfeit versions of these beautiful gifts. That's why the merry-go-round never stops. That's why love isn't lasting. That's why marriages are ending in divorce. That's why sex isn't respected or cherished anymore.

Embracing God's plan for love, marriage, and sex will radically change your life.

If we want to experience God's good design in these areas, we have to do things His way. We have to embrace His good plan. Get ready though. Embracing God's plan for love, marriage, and sex will radically change your life. It will change the way you live as a single woman. It will change the way you view your sexuality. It will change the type of guy you choose to marry. It will change the way you love your future husband. It will change the way you glorify God.

God's ways truly are the best ways. May we be a generation of women who choose to love sacrificially, marry permanently, and enjoy sexual intimacy within the beautiful covenant of marriage.

CHAPTER 5

STUDY GUIDE

"Whether a woman is single or married,
her greatest needs will only be met
when she's faithfully walking
in a relationship with Christ."

1. What did you find most interesting about the first love story of all time (Adam and Eve in Gen. 2)?

   _____

   _____

   _____

2. Circle the top three areas that have most influenced your view of love, marriage, and sex:

Chick flicks	Christian Romance Novels	Parents
Friends	Searching the Internet	School
Boyfriend	Nonfiction Books	The Bible
Youth Group	Summer Camp	Magazines
Conferences	Social Media	Internet Videos
Music	Pornography	TV

3. What does Genesis 2:24–25 teach about love, marriage, and sex? "Therefore a man shall leave his father and his mother and hold fast to his wife, and they shall become one flesh.

And the man [Adam] and his wife [Eve] were naked and were not ashamed."

_____

_____

_____

4. Write out your key takeaway for each of these areas:

   Love defined by God
   Marriage defined by God
   Sex defined by God

   _____

   _____

   _____

5. What are the biggest differences you see between God's design and purpose for sex and what the culture portrays?

   _____

   _____

   _____

MAKE IT *personal*

Grab your Bible and turn to Genesis 2. Take a few minutes to read this chapter and underline anything new that stands out to you.

6. TAKING FEMININITY INTO YOUR LOVE LIFE

Emily's big brown eyes beamed with excitement as she walked down the aisle toward her soon-to-be husband. This was her day. Her long-awaited moment. She was about to marry the man she loved and admired more than anyone in the world. She was about to become Mrs. Daniels.

When Emily first met her husband, Blake, she was twenty-six years old. They were both volunteering at a Christian music festival. Emily noticed Blake the moment he walked onto the stage. She admired the way he talked about God and shared honestly about his life. Emily knew she wanted to marry a man with that kind of passion for the Lord. In a quiet whisper only she could hear, she prayed that God would give her a godly man like Blake.

Emily ended up meeting Blake at an appreciation dinner after the event. She was impressed by Blake's character and heart for the Lord. Everything inside of her wanted to make the first move and secure a connection with him. She didn't want to lose her opportunity to get to know this amazing guy. She wanted to chase after him. She wanted to initiate. She wanted to follow her feelings. She wanted to jump on the merry-go-round.

Despite her strong desire to pursue him, she decided to hold back. She wanted to give Blake space to make the first move. To be the leader. To be the pursuer. To initiate. Before they left the restaurant, Blake suggested that the two of them exchange phone numbers to keep in contact. Emily excitedly agreed. And that was the start of their love story.

We Are Distinctly Feminine

In this modern day and age, women are not encouraged to handle romantic relationships like Emily did. We are not encouraged to allow the man to be the initiator or the pursuer. Biblical masculinity and femininity are rarely viewed as positive things anymore. We don't like the idea of the male and female having differing roles and distinctions in a relationship. It is often assumed that being different must mean being "less than."

Quite honestly, the topic of gender roles and distinctions can seem complicated and confusing at times. Questions like these are often tossed around: Are gender distinctions a good or a bad thing? Is one gender more valuable than the other? Am I weak if I enjoy being distinctly feminine? Am I spineless if I allow the man to be the initiator in the relationship?

He was intentional, just like in every other aspect of our lives, with His design for the male and the female.

If we, as modern women, try to answer these questions apart from the Bible, we will end up completely confused. If we use our personal opinions or preferences, we could answer those questions in a million different ways. Thankfully, God didn't leave us on our own to come up with answers. He was intentional, just like in every other aspect

86

of our lives, with His design for the male and the female. a purpose and plan that is better than anything we could come up with.

If we're willing to view our femininity through the lens of Scripture, our confusion will quickly clear up.

Like we talked about in chapter 5, the book of Genesis reveals how intentional God was in creating the male and the female. In those earliest moments, God could have created anything He wanted; He could have designed myriad gender types and human beings. But He didn't. In His perfect wisdom and love, He created two distinct genders.

.THEN GOD SAID, "LET US MAKE MAN IN OUR IMAGE, AFTER OUR LIKENESS. AND LET THEM HAVE DOMINION OVER THE FISH OF THE SEA AND OVER THE BIRDS OF THE HEAVENS AND OVER THE LIVESTOCK AND OVER ALL THE EARTH AND OVER EVERY CREEP-ING THING THAT CREEPS ON THE EARTH." SO GOD CREATED MAN IN HIS OWN IMAGE, IN THE IMAGE OF GOD HE CREATED HIM; MALE AND FEMALE HE CREATED THEM. (GEN. 1:26-27)

The significance of that last line should inform us of God's great intentionality: "Male and female he created them." God didn't create male and male. He didn't create female and female. He didn't create genderless beings. He didn't create a "choose your own gender" option either. With great purpose and care, He created male and female. Equal in value, distinct in function. He created us this way to be a reflection of a much more magnificent story. God created male and female to reflect different parts of His character and nature. And when we live this out, we bring God immense glory. As the book *True Woman 101* points out, "Men were created to reflect the strength, love, and self-sacrifice of Christ. Women were created to reflect the responsiveness, grace, and beauty of the bride He redeemed."[1]

When a woman chooses to take her femininity into her love life, it's a reflection of God's good and intentional design. And as we talked about in chapter 5, gender distinctions are a beautiful reflection of Christ and the Church. Marriage is ultimately a reflection of the gospel. Our femininity isn't really about us anyway; it's about us embracing this distinction for God's glory. Our friend Emily was a woman who understood this. She embraced biblical femininity out of a desire to glorify God with her life. She championed her husband's God-given role and supported his leadership out of a reverence for God's Word.

With great purpose and care, He created male and female.

As we say in our book *Girl Defined*, "When you welcome God's design for gender roles into your romantic relationships, you will help set up you and your husband (or boyfriend) for long-term success."[2]

So how can we, as Christian women, embrace God-defined femininity? How can we live this out in our romantic relationships? Here are four practical ways to bring femininity into your love life.

FOUR WAYS TO BRING FEMININITY INTO YOUR LOVE LIFE

1. LET HIM INITIATE.

I really like this guy, and I think he likes me too. But he hasn't made a move. Should I initiate something with him or wait until he initiates? I'm honestly worried that if I don't do something soon, it might not happen. —Kelly (age 24)

Questions like Kelly's are regulars in our email inbox. You've probably wondered the same thing. Should I take the lead? Should I make the first move? Should I initiate the relationship? In our modern culture, single women are told to be aggressive. We're told to "get out there and chase down that man."

However, when we look at Genesis 1 and 2, we see that God created Adam first and Eve second. God did this on purpose and for a purpose. As Elisabeth Elliot, one of the most respected voices on love and romance, says, "By the grace of God we have not been left to ourselves in the matter of who is to do the initiating. Adam needed a helper. God fashioned one to the specifications of his need and brought her to him. It was Adam's job to husband her, that is, he was responsible—to care for, protect, provide for, and cherish her. Males, as the physical design alone would show, are made to be initiators. Females are made to be receptors, responders."[3]

With that in mind, we would encourage a woman like Kelly to use self-control and restraint. Be patient and wait. Don't initiate and pursue out of fear of losing the guy. If the guy is truly interested, he will make a move. And if he doesn't, it's probably for the best. If this guy can't take the initiative now, he most likely won't in marriage. Trust that if he doesn't speak up, he may not be the guy for you—or the timing may not be right.

> Don't initiate and pursue out of fear of losing the guy.

Although it's difficult, don't manipulate things to get what you want. In your future marriage, you will want a husband with a backbone. You will want a husband who can take the first step and lead well.

Choose to embrace self-restraint and allow the godly men around you to initiate.

2. ENCOURAGE GODLY LEADERSHIP.

When I (Kristen) first got married to Zack, I was given a piece of marriage advice that I'll never forget. An older, wiser married woman told me, "One of the most powerful ways you can influence your husband is to be his greatest and most enthusiastic encourager." She went on to tell me about how some of the most impactful Christian men in history were also the reciprocators of the most beautifully strong and encouraging wives. Wow. I was inspired. Her advice stuck with me. I wanted to be that kind of wife.

Whether you're single or married, one of the most effective ways to influence godly leadership in men is through words of encouragement. Proverbs 16:24 says, "Gracious words are like a honeycomb, sweetness to the soul and health to the body."

Our words have the power of death and life.

Sadly, it's becoming less and less common to hear modern women speak a good word about men. We typically hear girls describe guys as dumb, stupid, lazy, out of it, clueless, and more. And even if the guy is lazy and out of it, calling him negative names probably won't inspire him to become much more. Imagine what a difference it would make to the men in our lives if we took time to compliment any ounce of good that we see in them. Proverbs 18:21 says, "Death and life are in the power of the tongue." Our words have the power of death and life. That's a big deal. The way we interact and speak to the guys in our lives will make a huge impact for good—or for bad.

If you're not sure how to begin encouraging godly leadership in the guys around you, here are some practical expressions of gratitude:

- "THANK YOU FOR HOLDING OPEN THE DOOR FOR ME. YOU REALLY STAND OUT AS A GENTLEMAN, AND I'M GRATEFUL FOR THAT."
- "I APPRECIATE YOU PRAYING FOR OUR GROUP TONIGHT. THANKS FOR INITIATING THAT."
- "HEY, THANKS FOR ALWAYS GETTING TO CHURCH EARLY TO SET THINGS UP. IT REALLY MAKES A DIFFERENCE!"
- "I JUST SAW YOU TALKING TO THAT NEW GUY IN CLASS. I'M SURE THAT REALLY MADE HIM FEEL WELCOMED. WAY TO GO."

Can you see the impact? Imagine if we all started dropping words of encouragement like that to the men in our lives. The choice is ours. We can use our words to build up or we can use our words to tear down. We can speak life or we can destroy. We can encourage godly leadership or we can diminish it.

Whether you are single or in a relationship, choose to encourage godly leadership in the men around you through your actions and words.

3. PROMOTE PURITY.

"Flaunt what you've got!" "Show off that hot body of yours." "Use it and own it." "Make him want you."

Phrases like these are totally normal in our modern culture. We, as women, are often encouraged to use our bodies to entice men. Magazines give us tips on how to be sexy. Movies show us how to be seductive and flirty. Music lyrics give us ideas on how to get what we want when we want it.

We are encouraged to use our femininity in manipulative and selfish ways. But that is completely against God's beautiful design for us. In Proverbs 7, God gives a straightforward picture of a sinful, seductive, and wily woman. In fact, the entire chapter is about a father warning his son of the type of woman he should flee from and avoid.

The Proverbs 7 woman is described as having smooth words (see v. 5). She is on the lookout for a man she can entice (see vv. 6–8). She is dressed seductively and is wily at heart (see v. 10). She is loud and wayward (see v. 11). She uses physical passion to allure (see v. 13). She prepares her room for a night of sinful pleasure (see vv. 16–17). She uses seductive speech to manipulate men (see v. 21). Her house is a pathway to death and hell (see v. 27). She's not exactly the role model we

> *Let's use our femininity to promote purity in the lives of the men around us.*

should be looking to. But she is exactly the type of woman our culture encourages us to become.

Instead of becoming Proverbs 7 women, let's choose to be women who reflect the holiness and purity of Christ. Let's use our femininity to promote purity in the lives of the men around us. As Psalm 51:10 says, "Create in me a pure heart, O God, and renew a steadfast spirit within me" (NIV).

Here are four practical ways to promote purity in your romantic relationships.

BODY LANGUAGE. You've got the beautiful body of a woman. Be careful how you present it. We, as women, know how to tilt our heads, swing our hips, or position ourselves in seductive ways that say, "I'm sexy and I want you!" Be careful with your body language. Choose to move your body in a way that isn't provocative (see 1 Thess. 4:3–5).

TOUCH. A woman's touch is powerful. When you touch your boyfriend, what are you hoping to accomplish? Are you treating him in a way that encourages purity? Make sure your interactions encourage purity and holiness (see 1 Pet. 2:1–3).

WORDS. We, as women, are good with words. We know just what to say to get our way. We know how to get our guy to do what we want. Instead of using your words for selfish gain (see Phil. 2:3), use your words to encourage and build him up. Use your words to promote purity and point him away from you and toward Christ.

CLOTHES. You have been given a gorgeous body. Dressing feminine and fashionably is fun! However, when you choose clothing styles, strive to dress in a way that draws your man's eyes toward your face. Represent yourself in a way that reflects the purity, holiness, and selflessness of Christ (see 1 Tim. 2:9–10).

When it comes to your femininity, choose to be a woman who promotes purity in your romantic relationships. Strive to build habits now that will make it easier for you to be that kind of woman in your future marriage.

4. POINT HIM TO CHRIST.

I (Bethany) met a godly young man a few years after my relationship with Justin. This guy was strong in his walk with God and I really enjoyed getting to know him. As the two of us moved forward into an intentional relationship, I carefully considered the influence I would have on this guy's life. I didn't want to waste my opportunity to be an encouragement and blessing to him. I genuinely loved him as a brother in Christ, and I wanted to do my very best to point him toward Christ. I wanted both of us to benefit spiritually from the relationship, whether or not we would get married. I prayed and asked God to use me to build him up and encourage him in his relationship with God.

Over time, it became clear that marriage wasn't God's plan for us. However, I can honestly say we both grew closer to Christ during our time together. This man helped me grow in my relationship with God, and he says I did the same for him. Our relationship wasn't a waste but rather a blessing because our focus was on the Lord.

You have been given a huge opportunity to influence your boyfriend and future husband to love Christ more.

Way too often we are consumed with our own needs, wants, and desires in romantic relationships. Instead of using our lives to point our man toward Christ, we draw his eyes toward us. We do our best to make sure the relationship revolves around us. We want to be the center of attention. We want our guy to be obsessed with us. We want to be his only priority and his greatest love. As we've explored in previous chapters, our goal in a romantic relationship should be much bigger than that.

You have been given a huge opportunity to influence your boyfriend and future husband to love Christ more. Take that responsibility seriously. Choose to care more about his relationship with God than your own personal happiness. Choose to make Christ the central focus of your interactions.

Be a Girl Like Emily

Taking femininity into your love life takes effort and intention. It won't automatically happen. When Emily first met Blake, she had to decide which type of woman she would be. Would she do things her way or would she choose to trust God? Emily chose to trust God by embracing these four aspects of her femininity in the relationship:

1. LET HIM INITIATE.
2. ENCOURAGE GODLY LEADERSHIP.
3. PROMOTE PURITY.
4. POINT HIM TO CHRIST.

When it comes to your romantic relationships, what will you do? Will you leave your feminine design at the door or will you choose to embrace it? The two of us encourage you to be a woman like Emily. Choose to boldly live out God's beautiful design for your womanhood. To learn more about biblical womanhood, grab a copy of our book *Girl Defined*. God's design for womanhood is truly spectacular. By taking your femininity into your love life, you will display a beautiful aspect of God's design that would not be revealed otherwise.

CHAPTER 6

STUDY GUIDE

"When a woman chooses to take her femininity into her love life, it's a reflection of God's good and intentional design."

1. Describe or draw an image that comes to mind when you hear the word *femininity*.

   _____

   _____

2. "Let him initiate" was the first way to take femininity into your love life. Using the scale below, how well do you currently do this?

   Not so well

   Okay

   Really great

3. "Gracious words are like a honeycomb, sweetness to the soul and health to the body." How does Proverbs 16:24 inspire you to encourage godly leadership in men?

   _____

   _____

   _____

4. How can you practically promote purity in these four areas:

Body Language _____

Touch _____

Words _____

Clothes _____

5. In what ways are you tempted to make yourself, rather than Christ, the central focus of the relationship?

_____

_____

_____

MAKE IT *personal*

It's time to encourage one of the men in your life. Whether it's your dad, brother, boyfriend, or husband, take some time to speak an encouraging word the next time you see him.

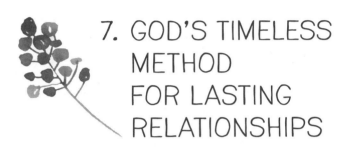

7. GOD'S TIMELESS METHOD FOR LASTING RELATIONSHIPS

"I really like him. Zack is such a neat guy!" I (Kristen) said to Bethany as we sat on the edge of my bed.

"Yeah . . . that's pretty clear. That huge smile on your face says it all. From what I know of him so far, he seems like a solid guy," Bethany said with a wink.

It had only been several weeks since Zack Clark expressed romantic interest in me, and I was trying hard to keep a level head. He was a wonderful guy and we connected on so many levels. I liked him. A lot. And the fact that Bethany "approved" of him too was huge. Because we were extremely close, her opinion and approval were musts for me.

As we sat on my bed chatting, our conversation turned toward the general topics of romance, relationships, and marriage.

"Relationships just seem so much less confusing now," Bethany said thoughtfully.

"Yes! I completely agree," I said. "We've come a long way. If only we had embraced more of these biblical truths when we were younger." I laughed. "That would have saved us a lot of drama."

"No joke," Bethany said, nodding her head in agreement.

With the clock pushing midnight, the two of us continued chatting long into the night.

It had been several years since our relationships had ended with Ryan and Justin. We had both matured a lot since then. Our perspectives on love and marriage were much more Christ-centered than they used to be. We no longer embraced certain aspects of the Merry-Go-Round Method. We no longer allowed our feelings to completely drive the train. We were done with the crazy spinning ride and were instead striving for something better. Something rooted in God's truth.

> God's truths were transforming our lives, and we were thriving as a result.

We were far from having it all together, but we were moving in a better direction. The more we embraced God's timeless design, the easier it became to navigate our love lives. Our thoughts became clearer. Our decisions became wiser. Our feelings became grounded.

God's truths were transforming our lives, and we were thriving as a result.

God's Timeless Method for Lasting Relationships

Unlike the Merry-Go-Round Method, God's Timeless Method for Lasting Relationships won't leave you sick and nauseated. Instead, you'll feel energized and equipped as you navigate your love life. You'll be driven by truth instead of feelings. Wisdom instead of infatuation. Trust instead of fear.

God's Timeless Method is also built on a five-step process, but as you'll soon discover, the steps are quite different from those of the Merry-Go-Round Method. This process is built on principles straight from the Bible. And as you'll see, God's Timeless Method won't leave you feeling nauseated after each ride but instead will leave you filled with wisdom and maturity. This method will help you steer relationships in a God-honoring way.

THE GOAL OF GOD'S TIMELESS METHOD = GLORIFYING GOD

Rather than being fueled by the goal of "personal happiness," the goal of God's Timeless Method is to glorify God in the relationship. Glorifying God should be the goal in every stage of the relationship process. From singleness to a romantic relationship to engagement to marriage, the driving motivation must be centered on bringing God glory. If you embrace the five steps but miss this point, you will have missed the most foundational piece.

When God's glory becomes the primary goal of any relationship, it informs the way decisions are made. It informs the motivation for purity, honor, and respect. It informs whether a couple should get married.

When the motivation of your heart is rooted in glorifying God, you will be ready to embrace the five steps of God's Timeless Method. These five steps will help you navigate your love life with truth, clarity, and wisdom. Since this

Glorifying God should be the goal for every stage of the relationship process.

method is built on biblical principles, it will produce immensely better results than the Merry-Go-Round Method. Whether your relationship results in marriage, God's method will leave you more mature and Christ-focused.

Throughout this chapter, we're going to unpack the five-step process for God's Timeless Method for Lasting Relationships, including how this biblical method works in real life. God's Timeless

Method has radically changed our lives, and we're convinced it will change yours too.

Let's jump into step 1.

STEP 1: CULTIVATE THE RIGHT HEART.

You're sitting in church when your eye suddenly catches a glimpse of a really good-looking guy. You stare at him for a few seconds trying to figure out if you've ever seen him before. *Maybe he's a new visitor*, you excitedly think to yourself. As your heart rate rises, you feel an intense urge to meet this guy. He's so handsome. And he's in church. How good does it get?

As your mind starts forming a post-service ambush plan, you're shocked back into reality by a sudden realization. You allowed this handsome guy—whoever he is—to completely hijack your attention and focus. You weren't even listening to the sermon anymore. You weren't focused on worshiping God. As you reel your emotions back in, you realize how quickly you were falling prey to step 1 of the Merry-Go-Round Method: *catch the right guy*.

Instead of embracing this wrong method, you redirect your thoughts and emotions back to God's truth. You remember how much more important it is to focus your attention on becoming a godly woman. You tune back in to the sermon and choose to practice step 1 of God's Timeless Method: *cultivate the right heart*.

As tempting as it is for us, as modern women, to focus on catching the right man, that shouldn't be our goal. When we make this our aim, we stop paying attention to becoming the right woman. We stop focusing on developing the right character. We take our eyes off God and instead put them on the guy we want. Remember, the primary goal of a romantic relationship is to bring God glory. Chasing down, initiating, and forcing something to happen with this guy wouldn't be a Christ-centered approach.

Instead of being on the hunt for Mr. Right, we need to be in the Word, becoming Miss Right. Our goal as single women should be centered on becoming more like Christ each day. We begin God's Timeless Method by seeking Him first.

Matthew 6:33 says, "But seek first the kingdom of God and his righteousness, and all these things will be added to you." This verse is saying that we should pursue Christ first, and when we do, God will give us what we *need* (not necessarily what we *want*). The context of this verse is actually quite amazing. It comes right after a bunch of other verses in which Jesus told the crowds not to worry or be anxious about earthly things. He exhorted the people and essentially told them to trust God by seeking Him first. He will take care of the rest. He will give them what they need.

> *Instead of being on the hunt for Mr. Right, we need to be in the Word, becoming Miss Right.*

That truth is just as powerful for us. As we seek to honor Christ first, we can trust that He will give us everything we need. We can trust that He is in control of our love lives. We can trust that His timing and provision are perfect.

Seeking God first is what it means to cultivate the right heart. We need to stop chasing. Stop forcing. Stop manipulating. Instead, we need to focus on becoming the godly women God wants us to be. We need to focus on cultivating hearts of patience, trust, contentment, surrender, humility, and selflessness.

I (Bethany) remember when I started practicing step 1 of God's Timeless Method in my own life. It changed the way I interacted with single Christian men. I wasn't obsessed with wanting to get their attention anymore. I wasn't focused on catching the right guy. Instead, I was intentional to interact with these men as my brothers in Christ. My heart was focused on glorifying God and my actions revealed that. The more I focused on developing the right heart, the more content I became.

101

Instead of focusing your attention on catching the right guy, God wants you to work on cultivating the right heart. That is the first and most foundational step in God's Method for Lasting Relationships.

Once your heart is focused on honoring Christ, you'll be ready for step 2.

STEP 2: CHOOSE TO SEEK WISDOM.

A guy you've admired for some time actually asked you out to coffee and you couldn't believe it. You've always thought he was a pretty cool guy. You know him well enough to realize that he is a solid Christian, but you don't know much more than that. As much as you've wanted to "catch him," you've exercised self-restraint. You've chosen to trust God. You've chosen to focus your energy on cultivating the right heart. But now . . . now! He has taken the initiative.

You agree to go to coffee with him and have a lovely time. He is even more of a gentleman than you realized. You're interested. Really interested. But you still don't know him super well. You can feel infatuation slowly taking over. You know how blind infatuation has made you in the past, so you determine to do things differently this time. Instead of coasting on infatuation, you decide to pursue step 2 of God's Timeless Method for Lasting Relationships: *choose to seek wisdom.*

You call your pastor, who happens to know this guy, and ask him some good questions. Then you talk to your parents about him and ask for their input and counsel. You then call your mentor (an older Christian lady from church) and ask for her opinion and advice. By seeking wisdom and counsel from the godly people in your life, you set yourself up for success. Moving forward slowly, you take one day at a time, welcoming regular feedback and advice.

Seeking wisdom from older, wiser people isn't something you'll see much of in modern culture. Flying solo is the way most young adults operate today. Coasting independently on infatuation is the default method. However, this is one of the worst things we can do in our romantic relationships. God did not create any of us to be solo fliers. He created us to thrive within community. Within family. Within boundaries. Within accountability.

God did not create any of us to be solo fliers.

Romance has a way of blinding us to obvious issues. Therefore, we desperately need outside advice to help us see clearly, to keep us on the straight and narrow, and to encourage us to live according to God's truth. If you don't personally know any godly women, the two of us highly encourage you to get involved in a local thriving, Bible-believing church. This is one of the absolute best places to meet older godly women. Be proactive and seek out these types of mentor relationships.

Proverbs 28:26 says, "Whoever trusts in his own mind is a fool, but he who walks in wisdom will be delivered." The Bible makes it very clear. If we trust in ourselves, we are foolish. But if we seek wisdom, we will be delivered. Delivered from what? Delivered from the consequences of foolishness. Proverbs 3:13 says, "Blessed is the one who finds wisdom, and the one who gets understanding."

I (Kristen) remember putting step 2 into practice during my relationship with Zack. Let me just tell you . . . it was hugely helpful. Zack and I both wanted to honor God in our relationship, but we knew how blinded we could become. So we intentionally chose to seek outside wisdom and counsel regularly. We constantly invited our parents' input into the relationship. We even asked them to hold us accountable to certain standards and boundaries that we had set up. We knew the tendencies of infatuation, so we welcomed outside wisdom to help us think clearly.

If you choose to embrace step 2 of God's Timeless Method, you will set yourself up for much greater success. With the wisdom of others, your eyes will be opened to things now that could have been hugely damaging down the road. You will see blind spots and areas of sin that could have gone unnoticed. You will see clearly whether it would be wise to continue moving forward in the relationship. Seeking wisdom is a good pattern to establish in your life now and take with you into your future.

Seeking wisdom is a good pattern to establish in your life now and take with you into your future.

Choosing to seek wisdom in your romantic relationship is the second crucial step in God's Timeless Method. Once your relationship is surrounded by godly counsel, you'll be ready for step 3.

STEP 3: CONCENTRATE ON GOD'S TRUTH.

The more you get to know this guy, the more you could see the two of you making a great pair. He possesses most of the qualities you've been praying for in a future husband. He's passionate about God and regularly encourages you in your spiritual walk. He's quite the catch.

Without you even realizing it, your imagination begins to run wild. You find yourself daydreaming about a future life with this guy. You see a white picket fence. An adorable little house. Cute kids playing in the lawn. And a white fluffy dog named Poochie.

You're feeling good. Really good. As your imagination continues to visualize the future, you suddenly experience an overwhelming urge to marry this guy. He's gotta be the one. He just has to be! As your feelings start to take over your brain, you pause. *Wait a minute. What am I doing?* you think to yourself. *Sure, he's an amazing guy, but I have no idea if we're going to get married. And the truth is, there's still a lot I don't know about him.*

And with that, you talk yourself back down to earth. You choose to reason with your feelings. You stop yourself from jumping into step 3 of the Merry-Go-Round Method (*concentrate on your feelings*). Instead, you choose to redirect your feelings back to reality and embrace step 3 of God's method: *concentrate on God's truth*. Choosing to concentrate on God's truth is another essential step for moving in the right direction.

Our feelings can be quite erratic. We can feel great about something one minute, then feel terrible about it five minutes later. Even though emotions aren't a bad thing in and of themselves, they tend to make terrible leaders. It will serve us well to harness our emotions with God's truth. Instead of letting our feelings drive our thinking, we must let God's truth drive both our feelings *and* our romantic relationships.

Psalm 119:105 says, "Your word is a lamp to my feet and a light to my path." Just as a lamp provides light on a dark path, God's Word provides direction for a romantic relationship. God's Word is *the* source of truth to guide the way down the relationship path. Instead of looking to feelings as the guide, we, as Christian women, must center our feelings on God's truth. Then, and only then, will we see clearly.

> Instead of letting our feelings drive our thinking, we must let God's truth drive both our feelings *and* our romantic relationships.

Our friend Sarah did an excellent job of concentrating on God's truth during her relationship with Matt (her now husband). As she was getting to know him, she regularly referred back to certain passages of Scripture for guidance and wisdom. For example, she looked at Philippians 4:8–9 and evaluated whether the relationship was marked by truth, honor, and purity. She read Ephesians 5:1 and looked to see if the relationship was pushing them to be more like Christ. She examined passages such as 1 Corinthians 13:4–13 and checked whether the relationship was built on God-defined love.

By looking to God's Word for instruction, wisdom, and guidance, Sarah made sure truth directed her relationship with Matt. Not feelings. This helped both of them keep Christ at the center of their relationship.

Studying God's Word and focusing on His truth are essential for navigating romantic relationships. God's Word will help you determine how Christ-centered the relationship truly is. It will help you make wise decisions when you're not thinking clearly. It will be your guiding light as you seek God's will. God's Word will help you determine if it would be wise to continue moving forward in the relationship.

Concentrating on God's truth is the third step in God's Timeless Method for Lasting Relationships. Once the relationship is centered on God's truth, you'll be ready for step 4.

STEP 4: COUNT ON CHRIST TO SATISFY YOU.

He brings you flowers. He opens your door. He makes you feel all warm and fuzzy on the inside. As your relationship grows deeper with this godly guy, your respect for him grows as well. You admire so much about him. He takes the initiative. He genuinely cares about you. He's sincere in his love for God. In your eyes, he's pretty amazing! Sure, he's not perfect. But he has a lot going for him.

As the relationship progresses, you begin to place more trust in this guy. Which is good. However, without even realizing it, you also begin to look to him for your satisfaction. You start to rely on him for your full emotional support. You look to him for fulfillment. You begin to place your security in your relationship with him, not in God. Slowly but surely, step 4 of the Merry-Go-Round Method (*count on him to satisfy you*) starts creeping into the relationship.

Thankfully, though, you notice this downward turn. Since you've been diligently pursuing God's Timeless Method for steps 1, 2, and 3 (*cultivate the right heart, choose to seek wisdom,* and *concentrate on God's truth*), you quickly realize your mistake. You feel convicted for looking to this guy for satisfaction instead of to Christ. You quickly realize how off track you were getting. You begin praying more diligently each day. You spend more time in the Word. You invest in your relationship with Christ. And as you do this, finding your satisfaction in Christ alone becomes easier.

As wonderful as this guy is, you know he can't meet all your needs. You know he can't fully satisfy you. You know he wasn't designed to give you what only Christ can give. And with that truth in mind, you make the intentional effort to embrace step 4 of God's Timeless Method: *count on Christ to satisfy you.*

Step 4 of God's Timeless Method is critically important for building a Christ-centered relationship and sustaining long-term, satisfying love. No guy can ever give you what only God was intended to give. No matter how amazing he may be, he can't cut it. Looking to a boyfriend (or husband) for total satisfaction is a dead-end road.

> *No guy can ever give you what only God was intended to give.*

Psalm 118:8 says, "It is better to trust in the Lord than to put confidence in man" (KJV). The original Hebrew word for "trust" in this verse is *chacah*. It means "to confide in, have hope, make refuge, (put) trust."[1] Instead of looking to a man for your hope, this verse is saying that it's better to put your hope in Christ. It's better to put your confidence in Christ. It's better to take refuge in Christ. It's better to find your security in Christ.

Since we, as women, tend to be much more relationally inclined than the average guy, it's tempting for us to look to humans for security. It's easy to place our satisfaction in our earthly relationships rather than in Christ. However, if we want to experience true and lasting satisfaction, we have to intentionally keep Christ at the center of our affections.

By looking to Christ for satisfaction, we won't be tossed to and fro by our emotions. We won't be shaken when our romantic relationship hits a rocky patch. We won't be devastated when our guy doesn't perfectly meet our every need. We won't be fearful and anxious in the relationship. We won't be ruined if it becomes clear that the relationship needs to end. We will be steady and confident in the Lord. We will be secure because our hope is in Him alone.

Applying step 4 on a daily basis isn't easy, but it is necessary for long-term relational success. It requires intentionality and discipline and daily time in the Word and in prayer. But it is definitely worth it.

Once you've applied step 4, you'll be ready to handle step 5 if it should occur.

STEP 5: CONTINUE TO TRUST GOD IF IT ENDS.

Not every romantic relationship leads to marriage. Sometimes the couple discovers deal breakers or red flags. Sometimes they just can't see eye-to-eye on something important. And other times there aren't any major issues, but their personalities just don't work well together.

Remember, our goal is to glorify God in the relationship, not simply to get the guy.

For whatever reason, many romantic relationships end. And as hard as this can be, it's not always a bad thing. Sometimes it's the absolute best thing. Remember, our goal is to glorify God in the relationship, not simply to get the guy. Sometimes breaking off the relationship is the most God-glorifying thing to do.

The two of us can attest to that. Even though we h[
through tough breakups, they were for the best. Looking back
now, we are so glad our relationships with Ryan and Justin ended
when they did.

If a breakup occurs (or needs to occur) in your romantic relationship, choose to embrace step 5 of God's Timeless Method:
continue to trust God if it ends. Trusting God is the key here.
And since you've been diligently applying steps 1, 2, 3, and 4 of
God's Timeless Method, step 5 won't be as challenging for you.
Sure, the breakup may be really (really) hard. But it doesn't have
to devastate your entire life. It doesn't have to steal all your joy. It
doesn't have to ruin your entire future.

Proverbs 3:5 says, "Trust in the Lord with all your heart." By
trusting God with all your heart, you're choosing to put your hope
in God. You're choosing to hold the relationship with an open
hand. You're choosing to trust that God's plan is better.

If your romantic relationship ends, go back to step 1 and repeat
God's Timeless Method again:

STEP 1: CULTIVATE THE RIGHT HEART.
STEP 2: CHOOSE TO SEEK WISDOM.
STEP 3: CONCENTRATE ON GOD'S TRUTH.
STEP 4: COUNT ON CHRIST TO SATISFY YOU.
STEP 5: CONTINUE TO TRUST GOD IF IT ENDS.

Unlike the Merry-Go-Round Method, God's Timeless Method
will grow stronger each step of the way. It's not about getting
what you want but about trusting God and seeking to glorify Him
throughout the relationship process. The ultimate goal isn't to land
a dream husband but to become a godlier and more Christ-focused
woman. Whether you ever get married, God's Timeless Method
will set you up for a life of trusting in Christ and finding total
satisfaction in Him. This is the goal we should always be pursuing.

Embracing God's Timeless Method for Lasting Relationships

And there you have it! God's incredible, awesome, and timeless method for lasting relationships. We hope this method is exciting for you. By applying this biblically based method in your life, you will be equipped to navigate your relationships with clarity, truth, and wisdom like never before. You will avoid so much of the heartache and devastation that comes with the Merry-Go-Round Method.

God's Timeless Method is so much better than Hollywood's. This method is centered on Christ. Built on wisdom. Grounded in truth. Pursued for God's glory.

As the two of us have applied God's Timeless Method in our own lives, our view of relationships has radically changed. We are no longer driven by the goal of personal happiness but rather by a passion to bring God glory. We're convinced that God's method will change your life if you faithfully apply it.

Come join us by embracing God's Timeless Method for Lasting Relationships.

CHAPTER 7

STUDY GUIDE

*"Whether you ever get married, God's Timeless Method
will set you up for a life of trusting in Christ
and finding total satisfaction in Him."*

1. List two specific ways that God's Timeless Method is different from the Merry-Go-Round Method.

   _____

   _____

2. Fill in the blank: the goal of God's Timeless Method =

   _____

   Why do you think this goal is so important to have?

   _____

   _____

   _____

3. Write out each of the five steps below.

   Step 1: _____

   Step 2: _____

   Step 3: _____

   Step 4: _____

   Step 5: _____

Which of the five steps stands out to you the most? Why?

_____

_____

_____

4. Thinking back on a past romantic relationship (whether yours or a friend's), how would have applying God's method changed that relationship?

_____

_____

_____

5. How can you begin applying step 1 (cultivate the right heart) in your life right now?

_____

_____

_____

MAKE IT *personal*

God's Timeless Method is something you can put into action right now. Write the five steps on a 3 × 5 card and stick it on your bathroom mirror so you can be reminded of these truths every day.

PART THREE

Single and Waiting to Mingle

8. WHEN YOUR HEART'S DESIRE IS UNFULFILLED

With my knees pulled up against my chest, I (Bethany) let my tears flow freely. *How could this be happening to me? How could I possibly be pushing my late twenties with no guy prospects in sight? Was long-term singleness really God's plan for me?* The questions, doubts, and worries rushed through my mind. The more I thought about my current state of aloneness, the more I cried. *Why?* I wondered. *Why doesn't God bring me a husband?*

Difficult moments like these have been scattered throughout the past few years of my life. Moments of wondering if maybe God had forgotten me. Moments of wishing God would take away this season and just give me a husband. Moments of wondering if I would be single for the rest of my life. Moments of wondering if my heart's desire would ever be fulfilled.

If you're currently single, I know you can relate to what I'm saying. I know you understand the confusion, worry, and sorrow that often occupies those lonely Friday nights at home. I know, at

Single and Waiting to Mingle

times, you've been the girl crying on her bed, wondering if things would ever change.

Unwanted singleness in any season of life can be really difficult and painful. I know, because I'm in that season. I get it. I'm in the same boat. I understand what it's like to have an unfulfilled desire for a relationship and marriage. I'm a solid ten years overdue in my expectations for when I thought I'd be married. The unfulfilled desire for marriage isn't easy to bear.

Unwanted singleness in any season of life can be really difficult and painful.

I want you to know that every word in this chapter comes from a heart of compassion and understanding. In writing this chapter, my prayer is that the words will be like a breath of fresh air and encouragement for you. I pray that you finish this chapter with renewed hope and a new perspective for your singleness.

Singleness Doesn't Have to Be a Season to Trudge Through

When I was single in my early twenties, I often found myself trying to endure my singleness. I would think to myself, *Once I'm married, life will really begin. Until then, I'll just try to get through these in-between years.* Without even realizing it, I began to look at married women as the ones who had "arrived." These women had left their single status behind and had officially begun real life. I envied their lives and counted down the days until my life would finally look like theirs.

After years of living with this type of mind-set, I realized that my perspective on singleness was all wrong. I was discontented and lacked joy. I wasn't living my life for God's glory. I was playing the waiting game. Waiting for Mr. Right to come along. Waiting for him to make all my dreams come true. Waiting for him to put a ring on my finger. Waiting for him to make me a complete

116

woman. Waiting for marriage to come knocking on my door so life could finally begin.

Thankfully, by God's grace, He slowly began working on my heart. Little by little my perspective changed. I began to see my singleness in a whole new way. God, in His perfect goodness, had a purpose for me in my extended years of singleness.

During this time of refocusing my heart on Christ, I came across some serious lies I'd believed. Lies about God. Lies about my worth. Lies about my singleness. Lies about marriage. Lies about the purpose of a relationship. Lies about my identity. These lies were subtly eating up my joy and tempting me to question God's goodness.

> *God, in His perfect goodness, had a purpose for me in my extended years of singleness.*

If you are struggling with singleness like I was, you're probably buying into some of the same lies. As you read through the following list, see if any of these lies stand out to you.

LIES VS. TRUTHS

LIE: I would be more valuable if I had a boyfriend/husband.
TRUTH: Nothing can add to my value. I am fully loved and valued as a child of God. "See what kind of love the Father has given to us, that we should be called children of God" (1 John 3:1).

LIE: I must have a boyfriend/husband to be happy.
TRUTH: True joy can only be found in the Lord. "'The LORD is my portion,' says my soul, 'therefore I will hope in him'" (Lam. 3:24).

LIE: My life doesn't really begin until I get married.
TRUTH: My life has already begun. I need to make the most of the time God chooses to give me whether I'm single or married. "Yet you do not know what tomorrow will bring. What is your

life? For you are a mist that appears for a little time and then vanishes" (James 4:14).

LIE: I can't be thankful until I have a boyfriend/husband.
TRUTH: Regardless of my circumstances, I need to give thanks out of a grateful heart for God's love for me. "Oh give thanks to the LORD, for he is good, for his steadfast love endures forever!" (Ps. 107:1).

LIE: God is good to other people, but not to me.
TRUTH: God loves me so much that He sent His Son, Jesus, to die for me. "For God so loved [insert name here], that he gave his only Son, that whoever believes in him should not perish but have eternal life" (John 3:16).

These are just a few of the lies I've believed in the past (and still do at times). I'm guessing you've believed some of them yourself. Maybe you can think of a situation or relationship where those lies specifically affected your life. Maybe you remember additional lies that you've believed in the past or currently believe. Our greatest fears and worries, as single women, can always be traced back to a lie. The more we fight off the enemy's lies and combat them with truth, the more content and satisfied we will become.

I encourage you to take a few minutes to think through the potential lies you've believed. Are they lies about God? Lies about your worth and identity? Lies about your value as a woman? Lies about marriage? Take some time to look up specific verses to combat those particular lies with God's truth. Exposing lies is the first step toward true contentment and genuine joy as a single woman.

A Woman Who Trusts

Throughout my years of singleness, I've found myself going back to a few specific verses in the Bible for encouragement. These verses always remind me of an important truth. A truth that we, as single women, regularly need to be reminded of. A truth that has the power to transform our single years into a season filled with fruitfulness and joy. What is this powerful truth? It's simply this: *trust in the Lord.*

The foundational struggle for most single women typically boils down to one thing: a lack of trust. A lack of trust in the goodness of God. A lack of trust in the power of God. A lack of trust in the love of God. A lack of trust in the sovereignty of God. And a lack of trust in the plans of God. The moment we take our eyes off Christ is the moment our hearts will begin to worry and doubt. If our trust in Christ is secure, our worries and concerns about getting married will quickly fade into the background.

> *If our trust in Christ is secure, our worries and concerns about getting married will quickly fade into the background.*

After my breakup with Justin, I really struggled with the idea of being single. I struggled to trust that God had a good plan for my future. I struggled to trust that God was really sovereign. In the weeks and months that followed my breakup, Proverbs 3:5–6 became my life anthem. "Trust in the LORD with all your heart, and do not lean on your own understanding. In all your ways acknowledge him, and he will make straight your paths." Those words became near and dear to my heart. I memorized them. Meditated on them. Prayed them. And asked God to make them true in my own heart. I wanted to be a woman who fully and completely trusted Him with my singleness.

Over the past few years, God has continued to use those words to point me to the truth. And that I'm still single today means I'm regularly putting those verses into practice. When I begin to feel discouraged, I remind myself to trust in the Lord with all my heart. Whenever I feel like life is going nowhere fast, I remember God's promise: "I will direct your path." Whenever

119

I feel confused or worried, I ask myself, *Am I acknowledging Him in all my ways?*

Getting to the Heart of Trust

Trusting God with your singleness is an essential step toward finding satisfaction. You will feel most content and joy-filled the more you surrender and entrust your desires to the Lord. Trusting God is one of the simplest but most difficult concepts to actually live out. I get it. Not an easy truth to apply.

> *Trusting God is one of the simplest but most difficult concepts to actually live out.*

To help you put your trust into action, the two of us created a simple and easy-to-memorize acrostic using the word *trust*. The T.R.U.S.T. acrostic is a great tool to help you unpack the meaning of the word. It's perfect to write down in your Bible or journal. It's helpful to read anytime you're feeling sad, depressed, uncertain, or worried about the future.

As a longtime single girl myself, this acrostic has been a massive help to me. If you're willing to apply the T.R.U.S.T. acrostic in your own life, it will be a huge help for you as well.

T.R.U.S.T

T—TURN

It's time to *turn* from sinful thoughts, such as worry, fear, and anxiousness. Don't allow yourself to fret about the future. I've done that, and it doesn't lead to lasting hope or satisfaction. Instead, choose to reject sinful thoughts and fill your mind with God's truth (i.e., God has a good plan, God is loving, God can be trusted, etc.). A great verse to meditate on is Isaiah 41:10: "Fear not, for I am with you; be not dismayed, for I am your God; I will strengthen you, I will help you, I will uphold you with my righteous right hand." Turning from sinful thoughts and instead counseling your heart with God's truth is essential in fully trusting in the Lord.

R—REMEMBER

The next time you find yourself in a puddle of tears, *remember* who Christ is. Remember that He is the same yesterday, today, and tomorrow. He never changes. He is the Most High God. The King of the universe. The Creator of everything. The Savior of the world. The One who is greatly to be praised. Remember His great acts of love for the Israelites. He rescued them out of Egypt and parted the Red Sea (see Exod. 14). He is the same God who protected Daniel and shut the mouths of the lions (see Dan. 6). He is the God who used a young shepherd boy to defeat a giant (see 1 Sam. 17). He is the same God who is alive, active, and in sovereign control over your love life. The more you remember His greatness, the easier it will be to fully trust in Him.

U—UPLIFT

Instead of whining and complaining about what you don't have, use your energy to *uplift* God's great name. Turn your whining into worship and start praising God with your whole heart. Choosing to uplift God's greatness is incredible medicine for the soul. The next time you are feeling down or discouraged, redirect your thoughts to uplift God's name. First Chronicles 29:11 is a great verse to praise God with and to worship His greatness. "Yours, O LORD, is the greatness and the power and the glory and the victory and the majesty, for all that is in the heavens and in the earth is yours. Yours is the kingdom, O Lord, and you are exalted as head above all." Refocusing on Christ and uplifting His name will help you fully trust in Him.

S—SURRENDER

Surrendering is one of the most crucial steps in the T.R.U.S.T. acrostic. Instead of holding on to your dreams and plans with a clenched fist, open your hands and surrender them to the Lord. Be honest with God. Share your heart with Him. Share your desires with Him. And then, surrender your plans knowing that He is all-loving and completely trustworthy. Trust that He will work out His will in His perfect timing. Psalm 9:10 is a wonderful verse to meditate on as you strive to surrender your dreams to the Lord. "And those who know your name put their trust in you, for you, O Lord, have not forsaken those who seek you."

T—THANK

Thank is the last and final word in our T.R.U.S.T. acrostic. When we choose to give thanks, we take the focus off our circumstances and place it completely on Christ. Giving thanks to God, concentrating on His goodness, and giving Him praise are some of the best things we, as single women, can do. Way too often we get so wrapped up in all that we don't have that we forget to stop and think about all that we do have. I encourage you to take some time out of your day to simply focus on giving thanks. Thank God for the many blessings that never change. Salvation, unconditional love, and everlasting life. If you're not sure where to start, begin by reading through Psalm 103. Here is the first verse of that passage to get you started: "Bless the Lord, O my soul, and all that is within me, bless his holy name!"

Living Out T.R.U.S.T.

Reading the T.R.U.S.T. acrostic is the easy part. Actually putting it into action is the difficult part. I (Bethany) encourage you to write down the acrostic and place it in a prominent place in your home. Read through it when you wake up each morning to help realign your heart with God's truth. If you are feeling down or discouraged, refer back to this chapter and reread through the verses in each part of the acrostic.

I totally understand that being single can be really difficult at times. I know there will be some really hard days in your future. Trust me, I've found myself crying on my bed plenty of times throughout my single years. It's not always easy. I have good days and bad days. Even with the ups and downs of emotions, feelings, and circumstances, I always come back to the word *trust*. I need to put my trust in Christ. I'm guessing it's the same for you.

Whenever you find yourself struggling alone, crying on your bed, or just feeling depressed about your future, stop and figure out where you are placing your hope. Is it in Christ or in something else? To realign your heart with God's truth, reread the acrostic and remind yourself of the five key words: *turn, remember, uplift, surrender,* and *thank.*

A Prayer of Complete Trust

I want to leave you with one of my all-time favorite prayers. It is by missionary and martyr Betty Scott Stam. This is a beautiful prayer of complete trust, surrender, and dependence on God. I have found myself reading it over and over again during this season of singleness. I encourage you also to read through it and make it your own. Pray this prayer to God and ask Him to make these words the cry of your heart.

"Lord, I give up my own plans and purposes, all my own desires, hopes and ambitions, and I accept Thy will for my life. I give up myself, my life, my all, utterly to Thee, to be Thine Forever. I hand over to Thy keeping all of my friendships; all the people whom I love are to take second place in my heart. Fill me now and seal me with Thy Spirit. Work out Thy whole will in my life at any cost, for to me to live is Christ. Amen." —Betty Scott Stam[1]

CHAPTER 8

STUDY GUIDE

"If our trust in Christ is secure, our worries and concerns about getting married will quickly fade into the background."

1. Which words best describe how you feel about singleness (circle all that apply):

Happy	Depressed	Anxious	Content
Purposeless	Excited	Worried	Joyful
Uncertain	Ashamed	Proud	Indifferent
Embarrassed	Fearful	Confident	Sad
Cheerful	Carefree		

2. Looking back at the list of lies vs. truths, fill in the lines below with additional ones that have been true in your life (make sure your truth is grounded in God's Word).

    Lie: _____

    Truth: _____

    Lie: _____

    Truth: _____

    Lie: _____

    Truth: _____

3. How can you apply Proverbs 3:5–6 to your specific life circumstances? "Trust in the LORD with all your heart, and

do not lean on your own understanding. In all your ways acknowledge him, and he will make straight your paths."

_____

_____

_____

4. Write down one way you can put each of the five T.R.U.S.T. words into action.

T—Turn _____

R—Remember_____

U—Uplift_____

S—Surrender _____

T—Thank _____

MAKE IT *personal*

Reread the prayer from Betty Scott Stam. Take a few minutes to write out your own prayer of surrender to the Lord.

9. FIVE STRATEGIES FOR THRIVING AS A SINGLE GIRL

I (Bethany) pulled into the overcrowded drugstore parking lot. As I walked toward the front doors, I felt as though I was wading through a sea of starry-eyed men and bouquets of red roses. With Valentine's Day just around the corner, it was prime shopping time. Flowers. Heart-shaped balloons. Teddy bears. Cakes. Dramatic, oversized cards. Chocolate-covered strawberries. People were snatching up these lovey-dovey items at lightning speeds. The grocery store looked like an explosion of red, pink, and hearts.

It seemed as though everyone in the store was in a hurry, except for me. I was just an innocent, single woman stocking up on my favorite drugstore mascara. As I stood in line waiting to pay for my makeup, the reality of my utter singleness stared me hard in the face. Another Valentine's Day was about to come and go, and I was very much single. No prospects in sight. No potential interests. No one on the horizon. No Valentine's Day date this year (except for my dog, Fluffy, but I don't think she counts as a true valentine).

Instead of melting into a flood of despair in the middle of the grocery store (like I would have done in previous years), I was surprisingly okay with where God had me. I had genuinely grown to fully embrace this unique season. The thought of being single on Valentine's Day (yet again) didn't depress me like it used to. I acknowledged my singleness, and I was totally okay with it. Hey, at least I would have great eyelashes. That counts for something, right?

Coming to this moment of complete joy, peace, and contentment as a single woman was a crucial turning point in my life. Instead of viewing my singleness as an in-between stage, I had grown to truly love and enjoy it. Instead of drudging through the Valentine's Day season (and despising the girls who had boyfriends), I had chosen to be a purposeful, productive, and Christ-centered woman.

> Instead of viewing my singleness as an in-between stage, I had grown to truly love and enjoy it.

As I write this chapter, I am still single. I don't have a boyfriend. I don't have a valentine. I don't have a man to whisper sweet nothings into my ear. It's me and only me. Even with my complete and total singleness, I can honestly say that I'm not just surviving this season, but I am genuinely thriving. And it's amazing.

I'll be totally honest with you though. I've been on both sides of the spectrum (surviving and thriving), and I know what they both feel like. Hands down, thriving is so much better. The woman I am right now is much different from (and oh so much better than) the woman I used to be. I no longer have to muster up a smile. I no longer have to force myself to choose contentment. Christ has truly given me a genuine peace and joy that is more satisfying than anything a guy could ever offer me.

FIVE STRATEGIES FOR THRIVING AS A SINGLE GIRL

Living in this state of satisfied singleness is exactly what I want for you. I want you to not only survive your single years but also genuinely thrive in and through them. Getting to this point doesn't happen overnight though. Over the past few years, I've come up with five strategies that have helped me thrive as a single woman. If you desire to do more than just survive your single years, these five strategies will help you as well.

1. LIVE ALL OUT FOR CHRIST.

We, as single women, have endless potential to make an impact for the kingdom of God. We have energy, often youthfulness, and the availability to invest in those around us. We have a certain amount of flexibility that married women do not have. We don't have a husband to help or care for. We don't have a marriage relationship to maintain. We can use those extra hours to pour into other things.

Instead of wasting our days waiting for the next season, let's live with purpose and intention. Let's take advantage of this incredibly unique season of life and live with eternity in mind. Can you imagine what our world would look like if we, as single women, lived all out for Christ? Imagine what would happen if we served in our churches, discipled the younger women around us, actively looked for ways to share the gospel, and truly valued Christ above all else. Our churches would look radically different. Our families would look radically different. Our neighborhoods would look radically different. Our cities would look radically different. And our world would look radically different.

As Kristen and I say in our book *Girl Defined,* "When forever comes, only the things you did for Christ will truly matter."[1] Let's choose to be single women who actively live with that in mind.

2. INTENTIONALLY GROW IN GODLINESS.

The ability to study God's Word and cultivate godliness has never been easier. We have podcasts, books, online sermons, and every form of advanced technology to help us grow. We have access to the teachings of nearly every great hero of the faith from the past and present. We can search the web for any passage of Scripture and find a great sermon series to teach us about it. The opportunities to learn are endless. We just have to make growing in godliness a high priority.

My car is one of my favorite places to learn and grow. Whenever I get in my car, I intentionally choose to listen to an audiobook or podcast. This time has been a huge part of my spiritual maturation. I encourage you to utilize your time to grow in godliness. Find something that works for you. It might be in your car, during your exercises, as you're getting ready in the morning, or something else.

> *"When forever comes, only the things you did for Christ will truly matter."*

After Kristen got married, she encouraged me to intentionally use my single years to grow. She said that the more I invested in my character now, the greater a blessing it would be to my future marriage. I encourage you to take her advice as well and invest in developing your character.

3. LOOK FOR OPPORTUNITIES TO SERVE.

Many needs exist in our churches and communities. Young women need godly role models and mentors. Elderly people are in need of love and companionship. Young moms could use a helping hand. If we open our eyes and start looking around us, it doesn't take long to find a need.

When it comes to getting involved and serving, way too often we wait until the opportunity comes knocking on our door. If the opportunity doesn't come knocking, we just don't do anything. Instead of waiting for opportunities to come our way, let's intentionally go after them. Let's proactively seek out opportunities to serve. If you notice a need in your church, be the first to volunteer. If you see a young mom who looks overwhelmed, offer to bring her a meal. If you meet a widowed older woman at your church, invite her to coffee.

Service is definitely a key strategy for thriving as a single woman.

I'm challenging you to actively look for opportunities to serve. Don't wait for someone to ask you. Serving others is one of the absolute best ways to get your eyes off your own circumstances and focus on loving others. Service is definitely a key strategy for thriving as a single woman.

4. EMBRACE THE UNIQUE ASPECTS OF THIS SEASON.

Don't miss out on what God has for you right now. Way too many single women waste these incredible years of opportunity. Don't make that same mistake. Live fully in the present.

I encourage you to do this by embracing the unique aspects of this season and making the most of it for God's glory. Take advantage of the opportunities to invest your time in things you couldn't do if you were married. For example, my younger sister Ellissa volunteered for a mission organization in China for several weeks during the summer. She realized that she's in a unique season of singleness that allows her the flexibility to do that. She's serving God in ways that might be difficult if she were married.

I encourage you to see your singleness through the same lens Ellissa is viewing hers through. Remember, God has you in this season for a reason. Take advantage of the unique opportunities in front of you and learn to view them as blessings, not curses. If you can view this season through that lens, then you will thrive as a single woman.

5. EXPAND YOUR COMMUNITY BEYOND ONLY SINGLES.

In our society, people tend to congregate by age and stage of life. Kids hang with kids. Teens hang with teens. College kids hang with college kids. Singles hang with singles. Married people hang with married people. Old people hang with old people. The groups don't mingle a whole lot.

Get outside of your normal friend groups and experience the benefits offered by those in different seasons.

Instead of restricting your community and friends to strictly singles, try mixing it up a bit. Spend time investing in those younger than yourself. Hang out with your grandparents or the elderly couples in your church. Get to know the families with young kids. Glean wisdom from couples who have been married for several decades. Get outside of your normal friend groups and experience the benefits offered by those in different seasons.

If you're willing to expand your community beyond only singles, you will mature and grow in ways you wouldn't have before. Expanding your community will truly help you thrive as a single woman.

Doing More Than Just Surviving

When I walked out of that grocery store packed with red roses and heart-shaped balloons that day, I was focused on these five strategies. My life was filled with opportunities to bless and serve those around me. Instead of focusing only on my desire for marriage, I was determined to serve God as a single woman.

If you're wondering what it looks like to live out these five strategies in your everyday life, here are a few ways I am doing that right now:

- ATTENDING WEEKLY BIBLE STUDY FELLOWSHIP MEETINGS.
- JOINING MY CHURCH'S YOUNG ADULTS SUNDAY SCHOOL.
- VOLUNTEERING TO COORDINATE THE WELCOMING COMMITTEE AT SUNDAY SCHOOL.
- BLOGGING, SPEAKING, AND WRITING FOR GIRLDEFINED MINISTRIES.
- DIRECTING THE AWANA PROGRAM FOR MIDDLE SCHOOL GIRLS AT MY CHURCH.
- MENTORING MY TWO YOUNGEST SISTERS ON A WEEKLY BASIS.
- KEEPING REGULAR COFFEE DATES WITH SOLID CHRISTIAN WOMEN DURING WHICH TIME WE ENCOURAGE ONE ANOTHER.
- LISTENING TO CHRISTIAN PODCASTS, AUDIOBOOKS, AND SERMONS TO HELP DEEPEN MY UNDERSTANDING OF GOD.
- READING CHRISTIAN BOOKS TO GROW IN MY MATURITY AS A CHRISTIAN WOMAN.
- PLANNING AND HOSTING GAME NIGHTS AND SOCIAL GATHERINGS FOR OTHER SINGLES.

These are some of the practical ways I've chosen to live out these five strategies in my own life. Feel free to steal some of my ideas, or come up with your own. You might have opportunities in your church or community that I don't have. The goal isn't to be doing the exact same things. The goal is to be doing *something* for God. Get involved. Get active. Get serving. Get focused on maturing as a single Christian woman.

> The goal is to be doing **something** for God.

The more you intentionally live out these five strategies, the more you will thrive as a single woman. And who knows, you might even have the courage to wade through the masses of starry-eyed men and red roses to grab your favorite mascara.

CHAPTER 9
STUDY GUIDE

*I want you to not only survive
your single years
but also genuinely thrive
in and through them.*

1. Which percentage best reflects how you're doing as a single woman (the total amount must equal 100%)?

   Thriving = _____%   Surviving = _____%

2. List one way you can apply each of the five strategies right now.

   Live all-out for Christ. _____

   _____

   Intentionally grow in godliness. _____

   _____

   Look for opportunities to serve. _____

   _____

   Embrace the unique aspects of this season. _____

   _____

   Expand your community beyond only singles. _____

   _____

3. Bethany shared some practical ways she is currently living out these five strategies. List three practical ways you can live them out in your everyday life right now.

   1. _____

   2. _____

   3. _____

MAKE IT *personal*

Get active doing something for God. Of the three things you listed above, choose one of them to put into action this week.

PART FOUR

Working through the Nitty-Gritty

10. HOW TO BE "JUST FRIENDS" WITH GUYS

Tears streamed down my (Bethany's) face as I vented my frustration over a fizzled friendship with a guy. "Why do friendships with guys always have to end this way?" I asked Kristen in frustration. "I thought we agreed to be 'just friends.' Why did he have to break our agreement?"

In that moment, I longed for the day when I would finally be married. I was sick of the drama, and I desperately wanted to graduate from this awkward stage of life. Trying to be "just friends" with guys (whatever that means) and balancing the never-ending "who likes who" drama is tough.

The two of us, like most girls, struggled with being just friends with guys when we were younger. Even though we were intentional about not casually dating around, it was still hard. It was still confusing. Despite the mutual agreements we made with guys, things always seemed to end in an awkward and frustrating way.

Then came the hardest day of all. The day Kristen left me in the dust of singleness and married Zack. It was a glorious day for her. She rejoiced that she was leaving the uncomfortable world of "just friends" behind. I wondered how much longer I would have to endure this confusing season. I mourned the thought of having a potentially long season of these relationships ahead of me.

> *Despite my desire to move out of the single season, God had different plans for me.*

Despite my desire to move out of the single season, God had different plans for me. Instead of continuing to struggle through the difficulty and confusion of being "just friends," I decided there had to be a better way. I didn't want to continue moving forward in an endless season of awkward "friend zone" relationships. In my heart, I knew there had to be a way to have appropriate, healthy, and God-honoring friendships with guys. I just wasn't sure how to achieve that yet.

Guy Friends Gone Wrong

I'll never forget the day I discovered where I had been going wrong. I was sitting in a question-and-answer session at a Christian conference on dating and relationships. On a piece of paper, I scribbled the question, "Is it possible to be just friends with guys?" I folded my note and stuck it in the big basket filled with dozens of other folded papers. During the session, my question was chosen. The answer the speaker gave was so simple and yet so incredibly eye-opening.

Although I don't remember the speaker's exact wording, I distinctly remember sitting in that session and realizing where my friendships with guys had been going wrong. In answering my question, the speaker encouraged us (the audience) in two key areas:

1. DON'T MAKE YOUR GUY FRIENDSHIPS ALL ABOUT THE TWO OF YOU. DO YOUR BEST TO KEEP YOUR FRIENDSHIPS FOCUSED ON GROUP SETTINGS. WORK HARD TO INCORPORATE OTHERS INTO THE RELATIONSHIP.
2. DON'T MAKE THE RELATIONSHIP DEEPLY EMOTIONAL AND FEELINGS ORIENTED. TRY NOT TO SHARE DEEPLY FROM THE HEART IN WAYS THAT WOULD DRAW YOU TWO TOGETHER IN AN UNHEALTHY AND EMOTIONAL WAY. SAVE THE DEEP EMOTIONAL STUFF FOR YOUR GIRLFRIENDS.

In the days that followed that conference, I felt convicted about the way I had not only used certain guys to satisfy my emotional desire but also been selfish in my interactions. Instead of making Christ the center of those friendships, I often made myself the center. I wanted the attention. I wanted the focus. I wanted to feel special and valued. Out of selfishness and convenience, I had used those friendships to make myself feel good. I excused my actions by saying, "We're just friends," and then I'd allow those friendships to go down a not so "just friends" road.

As I thought about what the speaker said, I realized that being just friends with guys was possible. I simply needed to make some serious changes in my heart and actions. I needed to be intentional about keeping those friendships in group settings and avoiding making those relationships deeply emotional.

Getting to the Heart of Being Just Friends

The two of us strongly believe it is possible for single women to have male friends. With the right heart attitude, wise boundaries in place, and a true desire to honor Christ, guy/girl friendships can be encouraging and beneficial.

When it comes to being friends with guys, single women tend to take two different approaches. Some women run away from guys. This is the group that huddles together at social gatherings. They keep their conversations with guys short. They make no effort to befriend the guys around them. For whatever reason (it's different for each one), these women have decided that avoiding and ignoring guys is the best option for them.

Other women tend to take the opposite approach. They run toward guys (the two of us definitely fell into this category). This is the type of woman who has no problem walking up to a guy and capturing his attention. She's typically bold, flirtatious, and outgoing. She does her best to catch and keep a guy's attention. She thrives on being noticed and usually does whatever it takes to get the attention she craves.

The two of us strongly believe it is possible for single women to have male friends.

From the outside, both these groups respond very differently when it comes to the opposite sex. But when you dig a little deeper, you will discover that the women in both groups have the same underlying problem—*they are focused on themselves.* They are most concerned with what makes them feel happy and comfortable and give little thought to how to encourage and push the men around them toward Christ. They also typically don't focus on glorifying God through a healthy guy/girl friendship.

There is another group of women, though, that we have yet to mention. This group is often the rarest of the three. This is the group that I would love to see you part of.

The women in this third group have found a healthy balance of loving their brothers in Christ while maintaining pure and Christ-honoring friendships. These women have placed their whole identities in Christ. They don't ignore men. They don't chase after men. They don't use men to satisfy their desire for attention. They don't view men as their source of identity.

The women in this group are intentional in making sure their desire to honor Christ fuels their actions, words, and motivations.

They are careful to maintain group-oriented, Christ-focused, and less emotionally intimate friendships with men. These women aren't thoughtless or carefree. They are careful to protect their own hearts, as well as the hearts of the single men they interact with.

The two of us love the way author Joshua Harris describes guy/girl friendships. "God wants us to neither run from each other nor use each other as an indulgent pursuit or short-term romance. He's calling us to be firmly committed to biblical friendships. In brother-sister relationships, men and women spur each other on to godliness—they stand against wickedness together, they seek God together, they honor one another and grow in grace side by side."[1]

THE GUY FRIEND FILTER

Glorifying God should be the goal of every one of your friendships with a guy and your driving motivation as you evaluate your actions and check your heart. "So, whether you eat or drink, or whatever you do, do all to the glory of God" (1 Cor. 10:31). With this in mind, the two of us are going to show you how to actually have God-glorifying friendships with guys.

To do this, we've invented an easy-to-use filter called the Guy Friend Filter. This helpful filter will take you through five super practical aspects of your guy friendships. As you think through your individual friendship with each guy, answer—honestly—the questions based on each aspect. Be truthful about your thoughts and be willing to make changes to the individual friendships that need it.

Pause right now and think of one specific guy friend you have. Do you have one in mind? Okay, once you have a specific friend in mind, take your friendship through the filter. Once you go through all five parts, go back to the beginning and do this with each one of your guy friends.

1. HOW MUCH TIME DO I SPEND WITH THIS FRIEND (SEE EPH. 5:15-16)?

Stop and evaluate the amount of time you spend with this guy. Ask yourself these questions:

Am I spending many hours just hanging out with him?

Am I intentional to make sure the time I spend with him is group oriented?

Am I careful to make sure my time spent with him honors Christ?

Am I trying to find my identity and worth in the amount of time I spend with him?

Am I neglecting my girl friendships for my friendship with him?

2. ARE WE GETTING EMOTIONAL (SEE PROV. 17:27)?

Opening up, sharing deep feelings, and discussing personal topics can lead a "just friends" relationship down a dangerous path. Intimate conversations will create intimacy. Be careful about the type of information you share (as well as the information you are willing to receive back). Ask yourself these questions:

Am I cautious with the information I share with him?

Do I share personal and/or intimate things with him?

Do I pour out my heart to him?

Do I use him to satisfy me emotionally?

3. WHAT DO WE TALK ABOUT (SEE EPH. 4:29)?

Your conversations with single guys should always be pure and God honoring. Ask yourself these questions:

What topics dominate the majority of my conversations with this guy friend?

Do my conversations with this guy contain crude, sarcastic, or rude comments?

Do my words push this guy friend toward Christ or away from Christ?

Are my words edgy, flirty, and/or seductive?

4. IS THIS GUY A GODLY FRIEND FOR ME (SEE 1 COR. 15:33)?

When choosing a guy friend, carefully consider his lifestyle and actions. Just because he's a walking, breathing, and smiling guy doesn't mean you need to develop a friendship with him. Be wise about the guys you choose as friends. Ask yourself these questions:

Am I intentional about choosing godly guy friends?

Is my friendship with this guy healthy and beneficial?

Are my morals being compromised in my friendship with him?

Does this guy push me closer to Christ or pull me away from Him?

5. HOW PHYSICAL IS OUR FRIENDSHIP (SEE 1 THESS. 4:3-5)?

Many single guys and girls struggle in the area of physical touch and affection. Make sure your friendship is marked by purity and holiness. You should be encouraging him toward purity in your physical contact. Ask yourself these questions:

Am I self-controlled with my hands, hugs, etc.?

Are my physical interactions with him intimate or sensual?

Am I honoring my future husband in the way I touch this friend?

What kind of messages are my physical interactions sending to him?

Guy Friendships Done Right

The two of us would love to see more single guys and gals interacting in Christ-honoring and mutually beneficial ways. When done with the right focus, for the right reasons, and in an appropriate way, being just friends with a guy can be a beautiful thing.

I (Bethany) have so enjoyed my guy friendships over the past few years. Ever since I made the decision to be more intentional in how I interact with single men, my friendships with them have been a huge blessing. I have grown closer to Christ because of them, and I hope I've done the same for them.

Are my friendships with guys always easy and free of complications? No. Are there times I have to make adjustments or rethink my actions? Yes. I'll be the first to admit that I don't always interact in the perfect way. Because of my outgoing and friendly personality, I have to regularly check my heart and make sure I'm not being flirty or selfish. I have to honestly evaluate these friendships and make sure my own desires don't become the focus of my heart.

Your intentionality will help set up you and your guy friends for friendship success.

The two of us encourage you to do the same in your friendships with guys. Regularly evaluate your heart, motives, and actions, and make sure your goal is to honor Christ. Regularly take your friendships through the Guy Friend Filter. If you aren't sure about a certain aspect of a friendship, ask a wise woman for honest insight. The more time you take to intentionally think through your friendships with men right now, the better prepared you will be to catch issues before they turn into real problems. Your intentionality will help set up you and your guy friends for friendship success.

We challenge you to do the same thing Bethany did. Choose to put yourself in group number three. Don't chase guys down

146

and don't avoid them. Instead, view them as brothers in Christ and choose to love them in ways that genuinely bring God glory. If you're willing to put in the effort to interact with intentionality (even when it's hard), you will develop encouraging, God-glorifying, and truly blessed friendships.

CHAPTER 10
STUDY GUIDE

"When done with the right focus, for the right reasons, and in an appropriate way, being just friends with a guy can be a beautiful thing."

1. Have you ever had a "guy friend gone wrong" situation? What happened, and what would you do differently this time?

   _____

   _____

   _____

2. In what ways do you struggle to be just friends with guys?

   _____

   _____

   _____

3. When it comes to guys, do you tend to run away from or run toward them? What is your motivation or reason for acting this way?

   _____

   _____

   _____

4. Remember those two helpful pieces of advice Bethany learned about—*don't make your guy friendships all about the two of*

you and *don't make the relationship deeply emotional and feelings oriented?* Which one do you find most challenging to apply? Why?

_____

_____

_____

5. How did you do on the Guy Friend Filter? What changes do you need to make to have a more Christ-honoring friendship?

_____

_____

_____

MAKE IT *personal*

Are there specific steps of action you need to take based on your results from the Guy Friend Filter? If so, ask Christ to help you begin taking those steps this week.

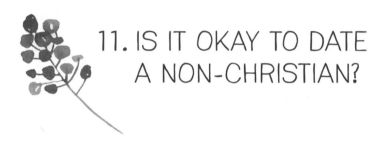

11. IS IT OKAY TO DATE A NON-CHRISTIAN?

"I met this amazing guy last week at school! We hit it off instantly. It felt like we had known each other our entire lives!"

This was the opening statement in an email the two of us received from a twenty-two-year-old single woman named Katherine.

Next she said, "After chatting for twenty minutes, he asked me out on a date. I said yes! And this is where things get tricky for me. After going out with him, I found out that he's not a Christian. And even worse—he doesn't have any interest in God. I really, really like this guy though. We totally click! But I'm not sure what to do. He asked me out on another date, and I really want to go. Do you think it's a major problem that he isn't a Christian? Please help!"

Emails like Katherine's are not uncommon in the GirlDefined Ministries inbox. We regularly receive emails with questions such as, "What's the harm in getting into a relationship with a non-Christian?" "What if he's a highly moral guy, but he's not a Christian. Is dating okay?" "We love each other and love is bigger than religion, right?" "He's not a Christian, but he's willing to go to church with me. Is that good enough?"

These are all great questions that demand solid answers. Maybe you've wondered some of these exact same things yourself. Before we unpack whether dating a non-Christian guy is a problem, we need to first ask this question: *What is the purpose of a romantic relationship?* Throughout Scripture, godly romantic relationships are always paired with marriage in view. The Bible never portrays a picture of a pure, Christ-honoring romance without marriage in sight. Why? Because romance isn't a standalone activity. It's a gateway leading us to an end destination—*marriage.*

As we've talked about in previous chapters, romantic relationships shouldn't be entered into casually but with intentionality and purpose. The goal of the relationship should be to discover whether God would have you marry that person. With this perspective in mind, we should be extremely careful about who we are open to dating.

> The Bible never portrays a picture of a pure, Christ-honoring romance without marriage in sight.

When it comes to dating a non-Christian, God's Word offers some helpful wisdom. As John Piper wisely points out, "The key text is in 1 Corinthians 7:39 where it says that a woman is 'free to be married to whom she wishes, only in the Lord.' That little phrase 'only in the Lord' is added to an otherwise innocent marriage to say, 'Don't go outside of the Lord to marry.'"[1] Basically, this verse is a direct exhortation to marry someone who is in the Lord (i.e., a true Christian). And since dating should lead to marriage, it wouldn't be wise to date a guy who isn't a Christian.

Here's another key verse that addresses this issue: "Do not be unequally yoked with unbelievers. For what partnership has righteousness with lawlessness? Or what fellowship has light with darkness?" (2 Cor. 6:14). If you're wondering what in the world "unequally yoked" means, here's what the passage is trying to illustrate: A yoke is a wooden bar that joins two oxen together as they pull a load. When one ox is larger, taller, smaller, or weaker than the other, it causes the team to lose all efficiency. They cannot perform tasks well. Instead of working together, they end up working against each other.

When it comes to dating or marrying a nonbeliever, the Bible says you will become like an unequally yoked pair of oxen. Basically, you're not a good match. You will encounter major spiritual differences, which will ultimately leave you spinning in circles. You won't be unified in the most foundational part of the Christian life—*living for God's glory.* The command in this verse makes it painfully clear that marrying a nonbeliever would be disobedient to God. This may seem harsh, but when we remember what marriage is ultimately supposed to reflect (the gospel), we will see how truly important this command is.

And if you're still not convinced, here are six major problems you will encounter if you choose to enter into a relationship with a non-Christian.

1. YOU AREN'T ON THE SAME MISSION (SEE MATT. 28:19-20; HEB. 12:1-2).

   As a Christian woman, you are here on a mission for God. He is your King. You are called to live for God's glory, to evangelize the lost, and to make disciples. A non-Christian boyfriend will not share this same mission with you because he does not serve the same King. You will most likely find yourself striving on your own with little support or understanding.

2. YOU CAN'T SEEK THE LORD TOGETHER (SEE MATT. 6:33; LUKE 10:27).

   As long as this guy isn't a believer, you will never be able to seek the Lord together. You will never truly pray to God together, seek wisdom from the Holy Spirit together, or learn from God's Word in the same way.

3. HE CAN'T PROVIDE SPIRITUAL LEADERSHIP (SEE HEB. 3:13; 10:24; TITUS 1).

God calls men to be spiritual leaders, and a non-Christian cannot provide that for you. No matter how nice or moral he is, he cannot provide you with spiritual leadership, because he doesn't have a relationship with God.

4. YOU WON'T SHARE THE SAME STANDARDS AND CONVICTIONS (SEE ROM. 8:7-8; HEB. 11:6).

No matter how you slice it, a non-Christian will struggle to share your same biblically based standards. Whether you are discussing the topic of purity, media choices, activities, language, or something else, you will regularly find yourself at odds with each other.

5. YOU WON'T SHARE THE SAME WORLDVIEW (SEE ROM. 12:2; 2 TIM. 3:16).

Whether you are discussing politics, hot topics of the day, evolution, abortion, or something else, a non-Christian will view life from a totally different lens than you. His source for truth isn't God's Word, so his worldview won't align with God's in many areas.

6. YOU WILL FACE CONFLICT IN RAISING FUTURE KIDS (SEE PROV. 22:6; JOSH. 24:15).

If you choose to marry a non-Christian, your challenges will only get harder. Raising kids in a spiritually divided house is tough. Mommy will want to raise the kids to love the Lord, but Daddy won't. Mommy will want to take the kids to church, but Daddy will be indifferent. Your kids will never experience the spiritual leadership a father is called to provide.

The two of us hope these six areas have opened your eyes to the major pitfalls of dating a non-Christian. We hope you can see how truly unwise it is.

"Well, what about missionary dating?" you might ask. Or "What if I date a non-Christian but promise to not marry him unless he becomes a Christian?" To answer those questions, read closely the wise words of Candice Watters:

> Since the purpose of dating is to find a spouse and since believers are not permitted to marry unbelievers, we must not deceive ourselves into thinking it's OK to date—as long as we don't marry—unbelievers. It's simply too likely, and too common, that what begins as an innocent, friends-only, non-emotional, temporary form of relating, progresses into affections that long to be satisfied. You would not be the first to think it harmless, only to set yourself up for either a heart-wrenching breakup or faith-wrecking disobedience.[2]

Regardless of how nice, moral, or fun a non-Christian man may be, don't compromise on this choice. Obey God's Word. Heed God's warning signs. Trust that His ways are better. Place God first in your life. As hard as it may be to say no to (or to break off a current relationship), you will be thankful you obeyed God in the long run.

Obey God's Word. Heed God's warning signs. Trust that His ways are better.

And for the Christian woman who finds herself married to an unbelieving husband, we want to encourage her to obey God's Word by staying faithful to her marriage (see 1 Cor. 7:12–14). As hard as such an arrangement may be, 1 Peter 3:1–2 offers hope to these wives. "Likewise, wives, be subject to your own husbands, so that even if some do not obey the word, they may be won without a word by the conduct of their wives, when they see your respectful and pure conduct."[3]

CHAPTER 11

STUDY GUIDE

"When it comes to dating or marrying a nonbeliever, the Bible says you will become like an unequally yoked pair of oxen. Basically, you're not a good match."

1. Based on this chapter, describe in your own words why it is unwise to date a nonbeliever.

   _____

   _____

   _____

2. How does 2 Corinthians 6:14 affect your decision whether to date a non-Christian guy?

   _____

   _____

   _____

3. In the space below, draw a picture of what you think an unequally yoked pair of oxen would look like.

4. Without looking back in the book, see if you can complete the sentence for each of the six problem areas listed below:

    1. You aren't on the same _____.
    2. You can't seek the Lord _____.
    3. He can't provide spiritual _____.
    4. You won't share the same standards and _____.
    5. You won't share the same _____.
    6. You will face conflict in raising future _____.

    What additional problem areas can you add to the list? Come up with at least two more.

    _____

    _____

    _____

5. According to what we explored in this chapter, is marrying a non-Christian man in line with or opposed to God's Word?

    _____

    _____

    _____

MAKE IT *personal*

Write out a short prayer asking God to give you strength to obey Him in this area of your life.

12. QUALITIES TO LOOK FOR IN A FUTURE HUSBAND

With giddy smiles on our faces, the two of us were doing our summer break right. As young teenage girls we knew the ingredients for having a good time. Just add the topic of cute boys to any conversation and life instantly turned into a laughter-filled party.

We would literally spend hour upon hour sitting on our parents' bed playing our favorite game. What was it? None other than the "pick your future husband out of the magazine" game. Oh, how we loved playing this. We would grab a stack of our mom's department store magazines and then open them up one by one. We would turn to the first page that had guys on it. And then we would take turns going back and forth picking out our future husband. There was a catch though. We could each pick only one guy per magazine. That meant no overlaps and no picking the same guys. Oh, the heartbreak! Just imagine the drama when one of us picked the "cutest guy" and left the other with second best. Thankfully, we didn't get into too many sister fights during our little game. We mostly giggled and squealed over the thought of marrying one of those cute department store models. Looking back now, we laugh about our teenage ways. If only real life were that simple. Open a magazine. Flip the page. Pick a cute guy. And—voilà!—your perfect husband appears. Unfortunately, real life isn't quite that easy. Choosing a husband requires a lot more wisdom than picking the cutest model in a magazine.

More Than a Cute Guy

Choosing a husband will be one of the biggest decisions you will ever make. This will be the man you will spend the rest of your life with. You will fall asleep next to him at night. Wake up next to him in the morning. Spend holidays together. Raise children together. Be grandparents together. Create your best memories together. Share your hardest moments together. You will spiritually be, as Genesis 2:24 says, "one flesh."

Taking this life-altering decision lightly is one of the worst things you can do for yourself. Choosing who to marry is a decision that should carry a lot of weight.

Choosing who to marry is a decision that should carry a lot of weight.

The two of us are grateful for the wisdom and input our parents gave to us throughout our teenage years. They regularly encouraged us to consider the type of man we wanted to marry. They challenged us to think about our lives ten, twenty, and even forty years into the future. What would we value in a future husband way down the road? What qualities would we want in a father to our future children? Would cute looks and a hot body be our number one priority? Or would we long for something more substantial?

As one author says, "Most married women desire their men to be godly, to have a good sense of humor (life is tough—laughing helps), to be an involved dad, to have a strong work ethic. And yet those four qualities sometimes take a backseat with single women."[1] Instead of living shortsighted and marrying for shallow reasons (e.g., he's cute, looks good in boots, and has nice muscles), let's think ahead and choose wisely.

Three Must-Have Qualities to Look For in a Future Husband

When it comes to getting married, we all have our ideal future husband in mind. We all have our own preferences, priorities, and things that really matter to us. I (Kristen) had a few preferences of my own. I wanted to marry a guy who genuinely loved God with all his heart, soul, mind, and strength. I wanted my future husband to have a serious desire to follow God. If I was going to follow my husband, I wanted to know he was reporting to a higher authority than himself. And . . . on the more shallow side, I really wanted to marry a guy who was taller than I am (c'mon, I'm 6'1"!). And for some reason I was more attracted to guys with slim noses (silly, I know).

> *I wanted my future husband to have a serious desire to follow God.*

I (Bethany) have had my fair share of future husband preferences over the years. As a single girl, with no husband on the horizon, I've had plenty of time to think through what I most value. To be totally honest, marrying a man with solid character and a love for the Lord grows in importance with each passing year. I also desire to marry a man who deeply loves Jesus and wants to use his life to point others toward Him.

The two of us could go on and on, sharing with you a long list of qualities to look for in a future husband. We could go through detail after detail, explaining the importance of each quality. As helpful as that might be, we've decided to keep it simple, short, and easy to remember. We're going to give you three must-have qualities to look for. Knowing these three qualities will enable you to look at any guy and figure out if he is potential husband material. Let's jump into the first quality.

LOOK FOR A MAN WITH VISION

If you are considering a man as a potential husband, you need to have a clear understanding of his spiritual vision. How is he going to lead you (and do it well) if he doesn't have a spiritual vision for his family? A man considering marriage doesn't need to have every single tiny detail of his life together, but he does need to have a vision for where he is going and where he wants to lead you, his wife.

The Bible actually has a very specific command for husbands that we, as single women, need to keep in mind. Ephesians 5:25–27 says, "Husbands, love your wives, as Christ loved the church and gave himself up for her, that he might sanctify her, having cleansed her by the washing of water with the word, so that he might present the church to himself in splendor, without spot or wrinkle or any such thing, that she might be holy and without blemish." A husband's job is to wash his wife in the water of the Word. That basically means he needs to help her grow in her relationship with Christ. When considering whether a man is husband material, figure out if he has somewhat of an understanding about leading you in this way. That will help you determine his vision.

A husband's job is to wash his wife in the water of the Word.

If the person you are considering is all about having fun and partying on the weekends, that's not a great spiritual vision. And if he doesn't have any vision in mind, that's definitely not good.

When I (Kristen) first met Zack, I loved that he had a spiritual vision for his life. He didn't have it all figured out (no seventy-year plan with his burial site purchased), but he knew where he wanted

160

to go. He wanted to work hard to provide for his family. He wanted to minister to others. He wanted to do short-term mission work. He wanted to be involved in his church. He wanted to mentor and disciple young men. He had a vision to serve the Lord, and I knew I could get behind him and follow his lead. Here are a few practical questions you can ask a future husband prospect. His answers will clue you in to the kind of man he is now and the man he plans to be in the future.

- WHERE DO YOU WANT TO BE TEN YEARS FROM NOW?
- HOW IMPORTANT WILL CHURCH BE FOR YOUR FAMILY?
- HOW DO YOU SEE YOURSELF LEADING YOUR WIFE SPIRITUALLY?
- WHAT PRIORITY WILL MINISTRY HAVE IN THE LIFE OF YOU AND YOUR WIFE?
- WHAT KIND OF LEGACY DO YOU WANT TO LEAVE BEHIND?

LOOK FOR A MAN WITH PASSION

Men tend to talk about what they're passionate about. If they're passionate about football, they'll talk about it. If they're passionate about food, they'll talk about it. If they're passionate about girls, they'll talk about them. If they're passionate about the Lord, they'll talk about Him.

When it comes to a potential husband, you need someone who is passionate about the Lord. That doesn't mean he needs to talk about God every second of the day; it just means he needs to have a solid relationship with Him. Deuteronomy 6:5 says, "You shall love the LORD your God with all your heart and with all your soul and with all your might." Striving to love the Lord with all his heart is a foundational quality in a future husband. If he isn't passionate about God, then will he drive his passions toward something else? If God isn't the center of his life, then how will he lead and love you well? What will motivate him to want to stay by your side as you grow old? What will drive him to his knees and turn to God for wisdom?

If a man truly understands the gospel, and truly understands what Christ did for him, he will be passionate about Christ. If he's not passionate about his relationship with God, you need to know why. Why isn't he passionate about the Savior who gave up His life for him?

Choose to marry a man who is passionate about the Lord now.

Marrying a guy who is athletic, exciting, and flirty—but lacks vision—might seem fun when you're young and carefree. But think ahead. Think about your future. What about when you're sixty? Seventy? Eighty? What about when life gets hard? What kind of man will you want then?

Choose to marry a man who is passionate about the Lord now. This is a must-have quality in a future husband.

LOOK FOR A MAN WITH **PURPOSE**

Finding a man who understands his purpose is crucial. If your guy doesn't understand his God-given purpose as a Christian man, he will constantly wander and never find a compelling reason to live. He will never find true satisfaction in life and will always be on the hunt for greener grass.

Your man needs to understand that God created him on purpose and for a purpose. He needs to know his calling as a Christian ("Go therefore and make disciples of all nations" [Matt. 28:19], "You shall love the Lord your God with all your heart and with all your soul and with all your mind" [Matt. 22:37], and "So, whether you eat or drink, or whatever you do, do all to the glory of God" [1 Cor. 10:31]). If he fully understands the purpose for his life, he will always have a reason to get off the couch, put down the video games, and use his life to make an impact. He will always be motivated to live for more than himself. He will always have an occasion to work hard. He will always have an understand of how and why to obey God's Word.

Whenever I (Bethany) meet a man who seems like a potential option, I quickly try to figure out what his purpose is. I'm not looking for perfection. I just want to know what keeps him going. What do his days look like? What do his weeks look like? Does he understand his purpose as a Christian? Do his actions prove that he takes his role as a Christian seriously? The answers to these questions quickly help me determine if he is husband material.

Choose to marry a man who understands his God-given purpose.

Choose to marry a man who understands his God-given purpose. Whose very existence is marked by Someone greater than himself. Whose days and weeks are filled with a motivation to bring God glory. Remember, if he truly understands his purpose, his life and actions will prove it.

What Kind of Husband Do You Want to Spend the Rest of Your Life With?

When you imagine yourself married one day, what kind of husband do you want to spend the rest of your life with? If God has marriage in store for your future, the two of us pray that you will choose thoughtfully. Don't settle for someone who has the looks of a magazine model but doesn't have a heart for the Lord. Dig deeper and figure out where he is going in life. What is his vision? What is he passionate about? What gives him purpose? A man whose life is marked by these things and who lives for the Lord is the type of person the Bible regards as wise to marry.

CHAPTER 12

STUDY GUIDE

"A man whose life is marked by these things [vision, passion, and purpose] and who lives for the Lord is the type of person the Bible regards as wise to marry."

1. List a number (1–10) next to each quality below in the order of least to most important for a future husband (1 being the least important and 10 being the most).

   9 Handsome face

   5 Great personality

   8 Godly character

   2 Jokester

   3 Big muscles

   7 Faithful and pure

   6 Involved in church

   1 Party dude

   4 Romantic

   10 Loves Jesus

2. In your own words, what does a man with vision look like to you?

   _____

   _____

   _____

3. Why do you think it's so important to marry a man with passion?

_____

_____

_____

4. Matthew 22:37 says, "You shall love the Lord your God with all your heart and with all your soul and with all your mind." How should this verse influence who you choose to marry?

_____

_____

_____

5. Who is the most inspirational and godly man you know? Why?

_____

_____

_____

MAKE IT *personal*

Grab a journal and write down the following words: *vision*, *passion*, and *purpose*. Underneath each word, record a few sentences that best describe these qualities. Keep this list handy for future reminders, encouragement, and prayers for the type of man you desire to marry.

13. WHAT TO DO WHEN HE COMES CALLING

You've dreamed of this moment. As he walks toward you, your mouth goes dry. You've talked to this guy dozens of times after church—but something feels different today. Something big is about to happen. As he gets closer to you, your heart starts pounding.

He strikes up his normal, cheery Sunday conversation. He seems extra excited . . . maybe even nervous.

You chat about the sermon and the latest happenings. Then, he strategically changes the conversation. He shares how much he's enjoyed getting to know you over the past few months. He says he likes how much you have in common. Then he speaks the words you've been hoping for. The words you never thought you'd actually hear. With a smile that melts your heart, he tells you how much he admires you. Then he expresses how much he would love to get to know you better.

Your heart does a somersault inside your chest. You pinch yourself to make sure you're not dreaming. *Nope.* It's real. And it's happening right now.

He's Interested—Now What?

He speaks up. You're interested. You're both excited! Now what? That's the million-dollar question. What's supposed to happen next? How do you navigate from this moment into a God-honoring relationship?

Zack and I (Kristen) asked those exact same questions before we entered into our relationship. We sought a lot of wisdom and counsel. In the end, we discovered that there wasn't one perfect system we could apply (e.g., casual dating, purposeful dating, courtship, dateship, etc.). Zack and I weren't as concerned about what to call our "relationship process" as much as we were concerned about being *intentional*. Honoring God and being intentional were our primary goals.

In this chapter, we're not going to give you a step-by-step system for what your relationship process should look like. Every relationship will have differing variables. There's no one-size-fits-all mold. However, there is a wiser and more Christ-centered way to go about things. Our aim is to give you the bigger picture. We want to show you how to practically navigate your relationship for God's glory.

As we talked about in chapter 7, the goal of your romantic relationship should be to bring God glory (see Ps. 115:1). The purpose of your romantic relationship should be to discover whether you and this man should get married. And if you do get married, the goal of your marriage should be to display a beautiful picture of the gospel.

To accomplish that end goal, you have to be intentional now. Each decision you make will take you either closer to your end goal or further away from it. By choosing to keep Christ at the center of your romantic relationship now, you will lay a strong foundation for your future marriage. If this aspect is missing, your relationship will be built on sinking sand. You will become consumed with self. But by keeping Christ at the center of your relationship, your passion will stay focused on glorifying God.

Before Diving Headfirst

When Zack first expressed interest in me (Kristen), we both had the big picture in mind: *marriage*. Zack wanted to begin a relationship with me for the purpose of seeing if we were well suited for marriage. However, before I said yes to a relationship with Zack, I asked myself three important questions. Before you enter into a romantic relationship with any guy, I highly encourage you to ask yourself these three questions too.

1. IS THIS GUY A GENUINE CHRISTIAN?
2. ARE WE BOTH MATURE ENOUGH TO ENTER INTO A SERIOUS RELATIONSHIP?
3. COULD I SEE MYSELF POTENTIALLY MARRYING HIM?

If the answer to any of these questions is no, then it wouldn't be wise to enter into a relationship with this person. As we discussed in chapter 11, if he isn't a genuine Christian, then a romantic relationship with him is out of the question (see 2 Cor. 6:14). If you're both too young or immature to pursue a serious relationship with marriage in mind, it would be much wiser to wait. And if you truly can't see him as a potential husband, don't drag things out by entering into a relationship.

For Zack and me, all three questions were a green light, so we prayerfully moved forward.

Building an Intentional Friendship

After I excitedly said yes to a relationship with Zack, we started spending more intentional time together. We didn't pair off and immediately dive into romance. Instead, we built an intentional friendship, which was different from the casual, acquaintance-like friendship we had enjoyed in previous years. This was a really fun stage. We didn't know each other very well, so we started things off by simply getting to know each other's core values and beliefs. Since the relationship was at the beginning phase, we didn't want to cloud our thinking and judgment by being overly romantic. Our motto for this stage was "romance to a minimum, friendship to a maximum."

To embrace this, we purposely spent most of our time in groups or public settings. We intentionally involved our families and friends. We wanted the input and advice from those we trusted most. My dad also spent some good one-on-one guy time with Zack, getting to know him.

This early stage was important for us to find out if we were even interested in taking things further. We asked each other a lot of good questions. And we had a total blast doing it! We discovered what each other believed about God, theology, family, the future, success, values, convictions, and much more. These intentional questions really helped Zack and me get to know each other on a deeper level. When we came across things we didn't agree on (which happened more than once), we would dive into God's Word and seek outside wisdom on that issue.

The two of us encourage you to build an intentional friendship before you jump into romance.

After several months of building our friendship (and praying our brains out), we both felt confident about moving forward in the relationship.

In this modern day and age, the friendship stage of a relationship is usually skipped. Couples jump straight into romance and physical affection before building any sort of foundation. They isolate themselves from all family and friends. They seek very little outside wisdom. As a result, the couple begins to "feel" in love long before they truly know each other. This usually leads to regrets and backpedaling further down the road. As Gary Thomas says so well, "Romantic attraction, as wonderful and as emotionally intoxicating as it can be, can actually lead you astray as much as it can help you."[1]

The two of us encourage you to build an intentional friendship before you jump into romance. Get to know this guy on a basic level.

Here are some questions to ask during this initial intentional friendship phase:

- WHAT DOES HE BELIEVE ABOUT GOD?
- WHAT IS HIS VISION?
- WHAT ARE HIS PASSIONS?
- WHAT GIVES HIM PURPOSE?
- WHAT DRIVES HIM IN LIFE?
- HOW DOES HE SPEND HIS FREE TIME?
- DOES HE UNDERSTAND GOD'S PURPOSE FOR MARRIAGE?
- DOES HE VALUE BIBLICAL MANHOOD AND WOMANHOOD?
- DOES HE VALUE PURITY AND HOLINESS?
- DOES HE TREAT YOU RESPECTFULLY?
- DOES HE SURROUND HIMSELF WITH GODLY INFLUENCES?
- DOES HE SEEK OUT PERSONAL ACCOUNTABILITY?
- IS HE ACTIVELY INVOLVED IN A LOCAL CHURCH?

Those are just a few of the necessary questions you'll want answered. For some additional questions, check out appendix B (50 Questions to Ask Early in the Relationship) on page 249. You're looking not for perfection but for signs that he is genuinely pursuing God and has a strong biblical worldview. Once you've invested enough time into building a solid friendship, ask yourself a few big-picture questions. From everything you've learned about him, does he still seem like a good potential husband? Is he someone you could still see yourself spending the rest of your life with? Do you have spiritual unity? Are the godly people in your life in favor of your relationship? Is the relationship honoring to God (even behind the scenes)?

The answers to these important questions will help you determine whether it would be wise to continue moving forward in the relationship. If at any point during this stage it becomes apparent that he is not a good option, don't continue. Choose to end the relationship rather than dragging it out unnecessarily. Be courageous enough to break things off now.

Moving into a Serious Relationship

Once Zack and I had established a solid friendship, we naturally progressed into a more serious relationship. I could clearly see that Zack was a man of godly character and integrity. He desired to honor God in our relationship. He welcomed outside input and wisdom. He embraced the counsel of our parents and other godly people. For me, these were huge signs that Zack genuinely wanted to honor God. I wanted to marry someone with that kind of character.

This was an exciting and fun new stage. We continued to get to know each other, but now on a much deeper level. We asked harder questions that would affect our lives if we were to get married. We discussed things like future plans, career, views on gender roles, finances, and kids. We also dug into each other's pasts and shared about past sin struggles, previous relationships, and current strains. With honesty and transparency, we got to know each other on a more intimate level. These things were important for us to know in order to keep moving forward. We wanted to know as much as we possibly could.

Since no major red flags were uncovered, we kept moving forward. Our families were still really excited and involved. Everything was looking great.

As things naturally progressed, we embraced more romance in the relationship. Flowers, sweet cards, dinner dates, and more. However, we still kept physical contact to a minimum. Zack and I desired to remain pure throughout our relationship process (which is a lot easier said than done). We established some firm boundaries and commitments, and asked our parents to hold us accountable.

Our boundaries included things such as not being completely alone in a house together, avoiding late nights alone in the car, not kissing until our wedding day, and saving sex for marriage. Although we weren't without flaws, our physical boundaries helped us guard our purity and honor God (we'll talk more about boundaries in the next chapter).

This stage of the relationship process is vital. Getting to know your guy's heart is key. Get to know his past, his struggles, his failures, and his victories. Don't leave anything out. This is crucial for uncovering any red flags or deal breakers. Don't shy away from asking the hard questions out of fear. Remember, if having a God-honoring marriage is the end goal, you'll want to make sure this man is someone you'll actually want to marry.

Getting to know your guy's heart is key.

Can you embrace him and his past? What baggage (if any) will be part of your future together (e.g., porn addiction, past sexual relationships, drug/alcohol abuse, financial debt, etc.)? Where do his views come from regarding things like family, career, gender roles, and kids? These are just a few of the important questions to discuss during this stage. Continue to seek outside counsel and input. Surround your relationship with godly wisdom. Pursue accountability and establish solid boundaries.

Figuring Out if You Should Get Married

With a strong foundation in place, Zack and I were beginning to see green lights for marriage. He had the core character qualities I desired in a husband. I had the core qualities he desired in a wife. We shared similar visions, passions, and goals. We had a blast hanging out together. We both genuinely loved God and wanted to honor Him in our lives. We were on the same page regarding all major worldview issues. Our families were still supportive of our relationship. Everything was moving in a great direction.

Instead of jumping straight into engagement, we wanted to take one more intentional step. Just because we loved each other and wanted to get married didn't automatically mean we should. As one author says, "Just because you're 'in love' with someone doesn't mean you should seriously consider marrying them."[2]

Zack and I began to seek specific counsel about whether we should get married. We sought intentional "pre-engagement" type of counsel and input from godly couples in our church. Receiving input from godly couples and having them ask us specific and pointed questions was extremely beneficial. This phase was short but essential in making sure we were well suited for each other and had covered all the bases. We didn't want to wake up on the other side of marriage with any major surprises.

> *Just because we loved each other and wanted to get married didn't automatically mean we should.*

As your romantic relationship progresses toward engagement, seek out some form of pre-engagement counseling. This will look different for each couple. The key is to be intentional to meet with an older, wiser couple. You might even ask them to mentor you through this stage of the relationship. Ask them to give you any and all advice they can possibly give. Invite them into your relationship and be willing to go deep.

This season of the relationship is crucial for finding out if marriage should be the next step. If all lights are green, you should both feel confident and excited about moving toward engagement.

Saying Yes to Marriage

With the sun setting over the beautiful Texas hill country, Zack got down on one knee and asked me to become his wife. As a gorgeous diamond ring sparkled in front of me, I looked into his brown eyes and couldn't imagine spending my life with anyone else. With tears of joy streaming down my face, I emphatically said, "Yes!" After a big hug, Zack put the ring on my finger and we just stood there soaking in this incredible moment.

I knew, without a shadow of a doubt, that Zack Clark was the man I wanted to marry. He was the man I had been praying for since I was fourteen. He was the man I wanted to spend my life serving God with. My entire family loved him, and his entire family loved me. All our close friends were excited and supportive. All the counsel we received had pointed us toward marriage.

The next eight months were a flurry of wedding and life planning. As excited as we were about the big day, we wanted to prepare for life beyond the honeymoon. We wanted to prepare for the ins and outs of married life.

In preparation for marriage, Zack and I did some book studies together on how to build a godly marriage. We also asked our pastor if he could do premarital counseling with us. (Once you're engaged, I highly recommend asking your pastor for premarital counseling. There's so much to learn about marriage, and a godly pastor can help you and your fiancé prepare well. The counsel and advice Zack and I received from our pastor—who had been married for close to fifty years—was priceless.) This time of intentionally learning about marriage was crucial for us.

Then, on June 18, 2011, I walked down a long church aisle to my handsome husband-to-be. My heart was bursting with joy.

With all our friends and family in attendance, Zack and I exchanged our wedding vows. And then . . . the moment finally came that Zack and I had been waiting for. With nervous excitement, we shared our first-ever kiss. It was beautiful. As our friends clapped and cheered in support, our new life as a married couple officially began.

Our two-part honeymoon to Costa Rica and Colorado was incredible. Experiencing God's spectacular gift of sexual intimacy within marriage for the first time was a fantastic experience for both of us. As hard as the waiting was, it was definitely worth it.

As our first year of marriage unfolded, we continued to be intentional about growing together spiritually. We continued to seek counsel, read solid books, listen to helpful sermons, and study our Bibles together. Like any newly married couple, we naturally encountered our fair share of conflicts and disagreements as well. But we were committed to working through them. We were committed to growing in our marriage. The solid foundation we had built prior to marriage was hugely helpful in getting our first year off to a great start.

As your relationship excitedly progresses to engagement and then marriage, continue being intentional. You're about to enter a lifelong covenant that is unlike anything you've ever experienced before. Many couples spend most of their time preparing for the wedding day and very little time preparing for the marriage. But remember: don't ever stop learning and growing.

Don't ever stop learning and growing.

Don't neglect marriage prep for wedding prep. You need both. Marriage is the second most important decision of your life (after salvation), so take time to prepare well for it.

A Beautiful Love Story Starts Now

The relationship journey is a fun, exciting, and challenging ride. And it will look different for every couple. No two stories will ever be the exact same. As you seek to honor God in this area of your life, keep the big picture at the front of your mind. Where do you want to end up in twenty years? What kind of future marriage do you hope to have? The choices you make now will affect how things turn out.

Constantly remind yourself of God's true design for love, marriage, and sex. Ask God for strength to embrace holiness and purity in your relationship. Pray. Pray. And then pray again.

> *Constantly remind yourself of God's true design for love, marriage, and sex.*

If there's one word that we could leave you with, it would be *intentionality*. If you genuinely desire to honor God with your love life, then you must be intentional about every step of the relationship process. Be intentional about the type of guy you get to know. Be intentional in seeking wisdom and counsel. Be intentional with setting up boundaries. Be intentional in pursuing holiness and purity. Be intentional to pray through every step of the way.

By navigating your relationship with intentionality and wisdom, you will lay the foundation for a God-glorifying marriage.

CHAPTER 13

STUDY GUIDE

*"If you genuinely desire to honor God
with your love life, then you must be intentional
about every step of the relationship process."*

1. Near the beginning of this chapter you were encouraged to ask yourself these three questions before getting into a romantic relationship:

   • Is this guy a genuine Christian?
   • Are we both mature enough to enter into a serious relationship?
   • Could I see myself potentially marrying him?

   Why do you think it's beneficial to honestly ask yourself these three questions?

   _____

   _____

   _____

2. What did you find unique and helpful about Zack and Kristen's relationship journey?

   _____

   _____

   _____

3. Why is intentionality important throughout the relationship process?

_____

_____

_____

4. List four benefits you see from building an intentional friendship first.

_____

_____

_____

MAKE IT *personal*

Create your own list of intentional questions to ask to get to know a guy on a basic level. We'll help you get started . . .

1. What does he believe about God?
2. What is his vision?
3. What are his passions?
4. _____
5. _____
6. _____
7. _____
8. _____
9. _____
10. _____

14. ROMANCE WITHOUT REGRETS

"Oooh . . . let's stop here for a picture! This view is incredible," I (Bethany) said. Without hesitation, I jumped out of the car, along with Kristen, Zack, our mom, and our Nana. The five of us were on a little excursion to the top of one of the most beautiful mountains in the world. We snapped a quick roadside picture and then hopped back into the car. Slowly but surely, we continued making our way to the top of Grossglockner, the highest mountain in Austria.

Since our maternal grandma (Nana) is a native Austrian, we had been dying to visit her homeland for years. This was our first time there. Nana was born and raised in a quaint little countryside town called Saalfelden. Austria was more stunning than we had ever imagined. (Not to mention the outrageously delicious food. Oh . . . Wiener schnitzel, we miss you!)

As we continued making our way up the mountain, we began to see glimpses of the gorgeous peak. We couldn't wait to make it to the top. Our goal was to reach the top and enjoy the magnificent view.

As anxious as we were to reach the peak, we knew the importance of driving slow and staying on the path. There was no room for distraction or error. One missed turn and we would plummet thousands of feet to our deaths. We had to stay focused on the road. We had to stay focused on our end goal.

The five of us had never been so grateful for guardrails. Some of those turns were extremely narrow. But by sticking within the boundaries and complying with the road lines, caution signs, and speed limits, we were able to enjoy the ride. No accidents. No cliff diving. No missed turns.

After several hours, we finally reached the top. The view was absolutely breathtaking. The five of us will never forget that phenomenal Austrian mountain experience.

Avoiding Roadside Regrets

Reaching the top of Grossglockner was our end goal on that excursion. We wanted to make it to the top without any roadside regrets. As modern Christian women, we share a similar goal in our romantic relationships. We want to make it to the altar without any major roadside regrets. We want to reach our end destination (a Christ-centered marriage) without flying over the cliff. We want to enjoy the journey along the way.

In the Bible, God has given us a clear road map for how to reach the peak successfully.

To reach the top and experience the stunning blessing of a Christ-centered marriage, we have to embrace God's guardrails throughout the relationship journey. We have to honor God's caution signs and road lines. We have to heed the speed limit. We have to drive cautiously and with wisdom until we reach the top. Boundaries and guidelines are no longer viewed as a burden but as a blessing.

In the Bible, God has given us a clear road map for how to reach the peak successfully. He has given us specific instructions for how to get there without going over the edge. Reaching God's summit in our romantic relationships requires us to be intentional by pursuing three key things throughout the relationship process:

1. WORSHIP
2. PURITY
3. HOLINESS

Worship means to value and esteem Christ above all else. The more we understand God's great love for us and the price Christ paid for our sins on the cross, the more compelled we will be to live our lives for His glory. *Purity* means to pursue a heart and mind that are free from sexual immorality. "Sexual purity may be expressed by what you do with your body, but it is ultimately rooted in your mind, your heart and your soul."[1] *Holiness* means to live a life that is "set apart" for God's glory. As God's children, He commands us to be holy because He is holy (see 1 Pet. 1:16). Since God is the source of true fulfillment and joy, we will experience lasting satisfaction by striving to become more like Him. Our romantic relationships will glorify God most when we build them on a foundation of worship, purity, and holiness.

FIRST THESSALONIANS 4:3-5 SAYS, "FOR THIS IS THE WILL OF GOD, YOUR SANCTIFICATION: THAT YOU ABSTAIN FROM SEXUAL IMMORALITY; THAT EACH ONE OF YOU KNOW HOW TO CONTROL HIS OWN BODY IN HOLINESS AND HONOR, NOT IN THE PASSION OF LUST LIKE THE GENTILES WHO DO NOT KNOW GOD."

By embracing a heart of worship, purity, and holiness in our romantic relationships, we will not only avoid much of the heartache and consequences that derail most modern relationships but also set ourselves up to experience God's best. God's plan for purity and holiness is a blessing because it keeps us on the right path. The best path. It helps us reach the top. It enables us to experience the incredible panoramic view.

Saying No to Sexual Compromise

One of the biggest temptations and struggles that derails most Christian couples from reaching the summit is sexual immorality. Sexual compromise, lust, and impurity are constant tempters in any romantic relationship. Like plunging cliffs around every corner, sexual compromise is looming around every turn. Hollywood makes the "alternative" routes look really appealing too. Like the Fairy Tale Facade in chapter 2, the off-roading option looks enticing and seems adventurous. *One night of passion won't hurt anything. You're going to get married anyway . . . what's the problem with a little sexual fun? Those guardrails are ruining all your enjoyment!* The pressure to embrace sexual sin comes at us from every angle (not to mention the sinful desires of our own hearts).

God's plan for purity and holiness is a blessing because it keeps us on the right path.

Sadly, too many Christian couples decide to ignore the guardrails. They disregard the caution signs. They forget their end goal. They lose sight of glorifying God. Instead of reaching the stunning view at the top, they find themselves crashed on the side of the road. Or suspended over a cliff. Or struggling along with flat tires, a dented fender, and a cracked windshield. Ignoring God's plan for purity will not produce God-honoring, long-term results. As Gary Thomas points out in *The Sacred Search*, "The same thing that feeds chastity—love and respect for God—will feed sexual enthusiasm within marriage. The same thing that feeds promiscuity before marriage—selfishness and fear—will kill sexual desire after marriage."[2]

If you want to have a strong, pure, and holy marriage one day, you have to start building it now. A God-honoring relationship must be built on self-sacrificing love, not self-gratifying lust. "If your dating relationship is sustained by sin, what will sustain your marriage?"[3] If sexual sin and compromise are ongoing patterns in your current relationship, then they will most likely be the default patterns for your future marriage. *You don't want that.*

Ignoring God's plan for purity will not produce God-honoring, long-term results.

The reason so many of us, as Christian women, struggle and fail to embrace purity and holiness in our relationships is because we take our eyes off the goal. We zero in on the relationship instead of keeping our eyes on God. We begin to worship the *gifts* instead of the giver of the gifts (see Rom. 1). And when that happens, our sinful hearts are much more inclined to give in to lust and sinful compromise. When our motives become anything other than glorifying to God, we will quickly be lured away by our sinful flesh. "But each person is tempted when he is lured and enticed by his own desire" (James 1:14).

According to authors Sean Perron and Spencer Harmon, "We guard our hearts because we are seeking to worship God alone."[4] To embrace holiness and purity in our relationships, we must seek to worship God alone. We must steer our personal affections to loving God most. Our actions must be driven by our love and obedience to Christ. Only when we're worshiping and seeking to glorify our Creator will we be able to maintain genuine purity and holiness in our romantic relationships. By pursuing Christ first, and establishing a biblically grounded and positive understanding of sex, we can experience a beautiful romance without regrets.

If you've struggled to embrace purity in your own life and in your relationships, the answer isn't to simply "try harder"; it's to pursue a genuine heart change.

We need to go deeper to the only lasting way to change our hearts—take them to the radical, costly grace of God in Christ on the cross. You show your heart the infinite depths to which he went so that you would be free from sin and its condemnation. This fills you with a sense not just of the danger of sin, but also of its grievousness. Think about how ungrateful it is, think of how your sin is not just against God's law but also against his heart. Melt your heart with the knowledge of what he's done for you. Tremble before the knowledge of what he is worth—he is worthy of all glory. In the end, it's the joy and wonder of the gospel that will change you permanently.[5]

Once you've realigned your heart with the gospel, you will be ready to apply some practical strategies for pursuing purity. If your past (or current) relationships have been marked by lust and sexual immorality, don't let that be the course of your future. As mentioned in previous chapters, God offers healing and forgiveness for your sins when you confess and repent (see 1 John 1:9). God can redeem your future. You can choose to walk in purity and holiness starting today. The two of us encourage you to pause for just a moment and read appendix A in the back of the book. Then come back and pick up where you left off.

God can redeem your future.

THREE STRATEGIES FOR PURSUING PURITY

Okay. It's time to get really, really practical. The two of us know how hard the battle for purity and holiness is. Whether it's our thoughts, motivations, or actions, we face temptations and struggles just like you. It's not a piece of cake! We haven't succeeded perfectly either. We've lusted. We've compromised. We've failed. But with Christ's strength, we've continued to push forward. None of us will ever succeed perfectly this side of heaven, but we must continue to march on. When we sin, we need to be quick to repent, confess our sins, and get back on track. Worshiping Christ is the goal. Pursuing holiness is the goal. Pursuing purity is the goal. And with Christ's strength, we can be victorious. "But thanks be to God, who gives us the victory through our Lord Jesus Christ" (1 Cor. 15:57).

Throughout our past relationships, the two of us have discovered some helpful strategies for winning the battle for purity. By embracing these three strategies in your life, you will be much better equipped to win the battle.

STRATEGY #1: MEMORIZE SCRIPTURE.

God's Word is powerful. It's "living and active" (Heb. 4:12). By staying plugged in to God's truth on a daily basis, you will equip yourself with ammo to win the battle. If you haven't made it a habit to memorize Scripture, then we encourage you to start today. By memorizing specific passages of Scripture, you will be armed with the truth you need when temptation comes your way.

We're going to share four specific verses with you that have been hugely helpful to us. Write these verses down. Tape them to your mirror. Think about them constantly throughout your day. When sexual temptation comes your way, pray these verses back to God.

"CREATE IN ME A PURE HEART, O GOD, AND RENEW A STEADFAST SPIRIT WITHIN ME." (PS. 51:10 NIV)

"FINALLY, BROTHERS, WHATEVER IS TRUE, WHATEVER IS HONORABLE, WHATEVER IS JUST, WHATEVER IS PURE, WHATEVER IS LOVELY, WHATEVER IS COMMENDABLE, IF THERE IS ANY EXCELLENCE, IF THERE IS ANYTHING WORTHY OF PRAISE, THINK ABOUT THESE THINGS." (PHIL. 4:8)

"BUT PUT ON THE LORD JESUS CHRIST, AND MAKE NO PROVISION FOR THE FLESH, TO GRATIFY ITS DESIRES." (ROM. 13:14)

"FOR THIS IS THE WILL OF GOD, YOUR SANCTIFICATION: THAT YOU ABSTAIN FROM SEXUAL IMMORALITY; THAT EACH ONE OF YOU KNOW HOW TO CONTROL HIS OWN BODY IN HOLINESS AND HONOR, NOT IN THE PASSION OF LUST LIKE THE GENTILES WHO DO NOT KNOW GOD." (1 THESS. 4:3-5)

These verses are powerful. They're inspired by God Himself. The two of us have seen God's Word do mighty things in our lives. We've seen God's truth help us conquer lust and overcome sin. And we're confident it can do the same for you. These verses (and others) should be the anthem of your romantic relationship. And if you're in a relationship with a godly guy, he will be on board with this anthem.

The two of us want to challenge you to memorize one of those verses this week. We also have a surprise for you. To make this a little more fun, we've given you a beautiful cutout in the back of this book with these four verses on it. So grab your scissors, flip to the back, and get these verses in front of you.

STRATEGY #2: ESTABLISH BOUNDARIES.

Just as guardrails keep a car from going over the edge of a road, boundaries in a romantic relationship help keep the relationship on the road. Nobody *wants* to fly over the edge. But without proper boundaries in place, slipping off becomes a lot easier. Boundaries are essential. They help us get to our end destination safely. They help us stay on the path of purity.

But before we jump into specifics, we need to understand one very important thing first. Boundaries *must* be motivated by our love for Christ. Staying physically and mentally pure for the sake of purity alone isn't enough. If that's our end goal, we've missed the bull's-eye. Rules alone don't honor God. Our goal for purity and boundaries must be rooted in a sincere desire to glorify God. Bringing glory and honor to our King is what we're after here. And if boundaries can help us do that better, then by all means, let's embrace them.

Boundaries are essential. They help us get to our end destination safely.

Establishing moral boundaries in your romantic relationship is something you should do early on. Ask yourself this question: "When I stand at the altar on my wedding day, what regrets do I not want to have?" By thinking through all the potential regrets you *don't* want to have, you will have a clearer picture of what you're aiming for. For example: not many Christian women get married and think, *If only I had kissed more guys in my past* or *Too bad I didn't sleep around more* or *I should have looked at more porn*. No way. The majority of Christian women we've interacted with don't wish they had been less pure; they wish they had been *more* pure. Setting up boundaries now will help you avoid this type of future regret.

This will look different for each couple, but the end goal will be the same (glorifying God in the relationship). Zack and I (Kristen) sat down together and wrote out a list of specific physical boundaries. We both desired to honor God and pursue purity. Once we finished our list, we gave a copy to our parents, some of our siblings, and a couple of close friends and asked them to hold us accountable to them.

To give you a specific idea of what a boundary list may look like, here's a peek inside Zack's and mine. Ours isn't a hard-and-fast list for every couple but simply an example of what was helpful for us in pursuing purity.

Out of a desire to honor God and embrace His best for us, we (Zack and Kristen) are committing to be faithful, by God's strength, to the following boundaries during our relationship:

- *We will not have sex until after we are married.*
- *To avoid temptation and compromise, we will never be completely alone in a house/apartment together.*
- *We will avoid sitting in the car alone at night for long periods of time.*
- *We will strive to keep physical affection limited to side hugs, holding hands, and putting an arm around each other.*
- *To avoid sexual compromise, we have chosen not to kiss until our wedding day.*
- *We won't discuss anything related to sex and intimacy until after our engagement (and guided by our premarital counselor).*
- *We will not watch any movies or TV shows that foster sexual arousal and lust.*

Those boundaries (and others like them) were extremely helpful to Zack and me during our relationship.

Like I mentioned before, your boundaries may not look exactly the same as ours, and that's okay. Just remember, the goal is to honor Christ in every aspect of your relationship. As you pray through and establish specific boundaries, it might be helpful to ask yourself some honest questions, such as, What physical actions have the potential to be a temptation for me/him? What specific places and locations could encourage the two of us to compromise?

Are there certain types of media and entertainment that could tempt me/him toward lust?

Don't leave something off your list just because it's hard. Remember, you are in a battle for purity against your flesh and the enemy (see 1 Pet. 5:8). As Elisabeth Elliot says, "If there is an Enemy of Souls (and I have not the slightest doubt that there is), one thing he cannot abide is the desire for purity. Hence a man or woman's passions become his battleground."[6]

> The goal is to honor Christ in every aspect of your relationship.

The battle for purity (both physical and mental) is real. Our enemy is real. Be willing to be extreme now to avoid extreme regrets down the road.

We, Kristen and Bethany, challenge you to grab a piece of paper and start working on some boundary ideas today. Even if you're single, take some time to think through what type of boundaries you would like to have one day. Boundaries are a sign of wisdom, not weakness.

STRATEGY #3: SEEK ACCOUNTABILITY.

Setting up solid boundaries is essential, but that's only the first half. Anyone can have written boundaries. But actually abiding by those boundaries is the challenging part. And that's right where accountability comes in. It's not enough for you and your guy to write down boundaries. As quickly as the mutually agreed on boundaries are written, they can just as quickly be mutually compromised on. That's why outside accountability is so vital.

Heath Lambert, a biblical counselor and author, describes effective accountability as having three key elements: "First, you need to find someone who understands that the commitment to accountability is more than simply the commitment to meet regularly. They must be willing to take time throughout the week to pray for you, call you, answer your calls, and check up on you. True accountability also requires someone who possesses the biblical knowledge and practical wisdom to guide you toward purity. Finally, true accountability requires an effort to be committed in the long term."[7]

With the above elements in mind, ask a few godly people to hold you accountable to them. For example: you could ask your parents, your pastor, a wise godly couple at your church, or a godly older friend. You will have to reach out to them. You will have to take the initiative. This may feel a little awkward at first, and that's okay. Don't let that stop you. Be courageous.

Once you think of a few key people, send them an email or text message explaining what you're doing. Ask them if they would hold you accountable to your boundaries. Be specific about what that will look like. Do you want them to call you once a week? Do you want to meet up in person once a week? What type of questions do you want them to ask you? How long will each phone call and/or meeting last? How often should they reach out to you during the week? Will they be okay with you contacting them as needed throughout the week for prayer and advice? Think through the details, and then take action. For each person who agrees, email them a copy of your boundaries along with five to ten specific questions that you want them to ask you each time you talk. Strive to surround your meetings with lots of prayer.

Once you have your accountability partners in place, get your first meeting on the calendar. Don't ease into it slowly. Dive right in and get things moving. As the months progress, stay consistent with your meetings. Always seek to be honest with your accountability partners. If failure and sin occur in your romantic relationship, confess that sin openly and discuss whether additional boundaries would be helpful.

Remember, in all this, the ultimate goal is to bring God glory. Don't lose sight of that mission.

Keeping the Summit in View

In all of this, pray diligently. Pray long and hard every day. Pray for your relationship. Pray for yourself. Pray for your guy. Pray for strength, wisdom, and conviction. We serve a real and living God. He is the source of our strength and power. We cannot be victorious without Him. Matthew 26:41 says, "Watch and pray that you may not enter into temptation. The spirit indeed is willing, but the flesh is weak." Our flesh is weak. But God is strong. Prayer is the antidote. Surround these three strategies with constant prayer.

We serve a real and living God. He is the source of our strength and power.

As Philippians 1:9–11 says, "And it is my prayer that your love may abound more and more, with knowledge and all discernment, so that you may approve what is excellent, and so be pure and blameless for the day of Christ, filled with the fruit of righteousness that comes through Jesus Christ, to the glory and praise of God."

By applying these three strategies, along with daily prayer, you will lay a solid foundation for your future marriage. Remember, your goal is to glorify God throughout the relationship process as you journey to the top of the mountain. The view is so much more glorious from up there. Don't settle for a cheap, off-road sexual adventure that derails you from pursuing your main goal. Choose to embrace the guardrails, boundaries, and caution signs now. Always keep the summit in view.

In the end, the journey is much more enjoyable when we pursue God's design in our relationships. Worshiping Christ, pursuing a heart of purity, and striving after holiness are God's road map for building a Christ-centered relationship.

CHAPTER 14
STUDY GUIDE

"Our romantic relationships will glorify God most when we build them on a foundation of worship, purity, and holiness."

1. Describe a time in your life when boundaries, guardrails, limits, etc. were extremely helpful for you (it doesn't have to revolve around a relationship).

   _____

   _____

   _____

2. Add a short description for each one of these words:

   Worship = _____

   Purity = _____

   Holiness = _____

   Why are these essential for building a Christ-centered marriage?

3. Fill in the blanks:

   "For this is the will of God, your sanctification: that you abstain from _____ _____; that each one of you know how to control his own body in _____ and _____, not in the passion of lust like the Gentiles who do not know God" (1 Thess. 4:3–5).

4. List the three strategies for pursuing purity:

Strategy #1: _____

Strategy #2: _____

Strategy #3: _____

How could applying these three strategies be helpful in your life right now?

_____

_____

_____

MAKE IT *personal*

Spend a few minutes memorizing Psalm 51:10: "Create in me a pure heart, O God, and renew a steadfast spirit within me" (NIV).

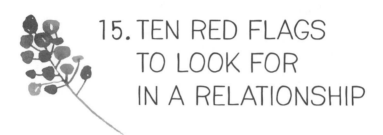

15. TEN RED FLAGS TO LOOK FOR IN A RELATIONSHIP

The red flags (i.e., concerns, problems, sin issues, major character flaws, etc.) were there, but I (Bethany) ignored them. I didn't want to believe that my hours upon hours of invested time could potentially come to an end. Instead of facing the facts and acknowledging the red flags in my relationship, I ignored them.

Why did I ignore the warning signs and problems in this relationship? Fear. I was scared. I didn't want to face the truth. I didn't want to think about my future without this guy. I didn't want to be single again. I didn't want to face starting over. I didn't want to deal with the pain of a broken heart.

Looking back now, I wish I would have acknowledged the red flags the moment I realized they were there. Ignoring them didn't save me from heartache; it only caused the relationship to drag on unnecessarily. More time. More heartache. More pain.

Eventually, I did face the red flags (after I grudgingly dragged my feet for several months). Instead of continuing to shove them under the rug, I decided to seek wisdom and brought my concerns to my parents. As difficult as it was for my parents to tell me the hard truth, they were honest. My parents were concerned about my future with this guy. After much discussion and prayer, they encouraged me to take some time to think, pray, and seek additional counsel. After seeking more counsel and praying fervently, I knew what I needed to do. I needed to end the relationship.

TEN RED FLAGS TO LOOK FOR IN YOUR ROMANTIC RELATIONSHIP

When it comes to red flags in our relationships, we, as modern women, far too often ignore them. We pretend they don't exist. We don't want to deal with the potential conflict, change, or emotional heartache that may come as a result of acknowledging them. We often choose to ignore the issues and move forward rather than dealing with the reality of our situation. As difficult as it might be to face the red flags, we need to remember that they serve a purpose—they warn us about potential danger ahead.

Looking back now, I wish I would have acknowledged the red flags the moment I realized they were there.

The two of us strongly encourage you to be honest about the reality of your relationship. Don't ignore your concerns and expect them to go away. Acknowledge the red flags for what they truly are and don't sugarcoat the issues. Use wisdom and seek outside counsel from a wiser, older Christian. They will be able to offer you insight from a nonemotional perspective and share honestly why you're having trouble acknowledging all the facts about the relationship.

Although each relationship will look a little bit different, there are some typical red flags to keep an eye out for. What follows is a list of ten of the most common red flags to look for in your romantic relationship. As you read this list, keep in mind that red flags vary in severity. Not every red flag is an automatic deal breaker. Each flag needs to be taken into thoughtful consideration within the context of the individual relationship.

1. HE HAS A SHALLOW RELATIONSHIP WITH GOD.

The foundation of your guy's life should be his relationship with God. He won't be perfect, but he should be growing in his spiritual walk. If your guy isn't spending time in the Word, isn't involved in church, and isn't seeking accountability, you need to double check his foundation. As we've talked about in previous chapters, that should be an automatic deal breaker (see 2 Cor. 6:14). If your guy has a weak and struggling relationship with God, be concerned. This should be the most important aspect of your guy's life. Take this red flag seriously. The ultimate red flag, of course, is if your guy is not a Christian.

2. HE PULLS YOU DOWN SPIRITUALLY.

A man who genuinely loves the Lord will naturally encourage you in your relationship with Christ. If he's doing the opposite by pulling you down spiritually, that's a problem. If being with this guy has weakened your relationship with Christ, that's a serious red flag. Remember, husbands are called to disciple their wives in the Word (see Eph. 5:25–27). If your guy can't encourage you in the Word right now, what makes you think he will do that in the future? Take your relationship with God seriously. It's the most important part of your life. Don't compromise your relationship with God for the sake of a relationship with a guy.

3. HE'S STUCK IN HABITUAL SIN.

Porn, lust, anger, alcohol and drug addiction, and gluttony are just a few of the habitual sins you might face in your relationship. Please understand that these habitual sins will not automatically disappear once you're married. Habitual, unrepented sin is a serious matter of the heart (see James 1:15). Until a person's heart changes, the sin will always reappear. If your guy is stuck in habitual sin, you need to stop and seek outside counsel. Don't push forward and naively hope it will disappear. It won't.

The two of us have seen too many women push forward and expect marriage to change their man. Marriage may hide the sin for a bit, but it will always come back. Don't be a woman who assumes she can change a man.

4. HE PRESSURES YOU TO COMPROMISE SEXUALLY.

If a guy pressures you to compromise sexually, he is not showing you Christlike, agape love. He's not encouraging you toward purity and holiness (see 1 Thess. 4:7). He's not striving to honor God in that area of the relationship. He's focusing on his wants and is sadly using you to satisfy them. He's being selfish and putting his desires above all else (see Phil. 2:3–4). Although it may seem flattering that he desires to be with you, it's not. He's choosing to sin and is willing to pull you down with him.

5. HE'S RUSHING THE RELATIONSHIP.

If your guy is impatiently rushing the relationship forward, this should signal your red flag antennas (see 1 Cor. 13:4). Stop and figure out why he's in such a rush. Why does he want to move so quickly? Is there a good reason for his rushing? Is he trying to snatch you up before his true character shows through? Time is your best friend in the relationship. Just because he's in a big hurry doesn't mean you have to be as well.

6. WISE PEOPLE IN YOUR LIFE DON'T SUPPORT THE RELATIONSHIP.

Wise people are in your life for a reason. Whether they're your parents, your siblings, a mentor, your pastor, or someone else, these people typically know you better than most anyone else. They often know your strengths and weaknesses very well. If the wise people in your life have major reservations about a guy, take their concerns seriously. Don't ignore them or disregard what they share with you (see Prov. 3:13). Even if you don't like what they have to say, at least hear them out.

7. HE HAS VERY FEW SPIRITUAL CONVICTIONS.

If your guy has very few spiritual convictions, you need to figure out why. A guy who is seeking the Lord, studying the Bible, involved in church, and striving to honor God will choose to live according to biblical truths (see John 14:15). If your guy lacks personal conviction in his life (i.e., falls prey to sexual immorality, drunkenness, dishonesty, etc.), a deeper issue most likely needs to be addressed. Instead of trying to force your personal convictions onto your guy, share the details of the relationship with a godly woman and communicate honestly about the lack of conviction in your man's life.

8. HE DOESN'T KEEP HIS WORD.

Every girl wants to marry a man she can fully trust. A man she can rely on. A man she can feel safe and secure giving her entire life to. When a man doesn't fulfill his promises (big or small), it

198

creates a serious lack of trust in the relationship. When your man says he is going to do something (e.g., spend time in God's Word, attend church each week, refrain from drinking too much, avoid getting into debt, etc.) but regularly breaks his word, that creates a lack of trust and shows that he is not a man of integrity (see Eph. 4:25). You need to be able to trust that your man will do what he says. If he regularly breaks his promises, that's a red flag that needs to be considered.

9. HE WANTS TO KEEP THE RELATIONSHIP A SECRET.

He says he loves you. He says he cares about you. He says he eventually wants people to know about the relationship. But for now, he convinces you to keep things just between the two of you. He wants to keep the relationship a secret. With the rise of online dating and communication, having a secret relationship is easier than ever before. If your guy wants to keep your relationship a secret from everyone, that's a major red flag. Why does he want to keep it a secret? Why is he afraid to tell people? Why does he want to hide it? The wisest thing to do is to bring the relationship into the light. Remember, there is wisdom in counselors (see Prov. 11:14).

10. HE'S OBSESSED WITH HIMSELF.

He's easily irritated. He's quick to find faults in others. He's obsessed with his muscles and outward appearance. He usually thinks of his comforts and needs before yours. His main concerns in life are his desires. He's just overly concerned about himself. If this describes your guy in any way, it should raise a red flag in your mind. If your guy isn't placing Christ at the center of his life, he will be consumed with himself (see Phil. 2:3–4). His priorities will be seriously out of whack. His obsession with himself will not magically go away once you're married.

Don't Ignore the Red Flags

As you were reading through the ten red flags, did any stand out to you? If they did, we are proud of you for having the courage to acknowledge them. That means you're still viewing your guy with a clear perspective. Infatuation hasn't totally taken over and you're still able to honestly evaluate the relationship. At this point the most important thing you can do is to seek outside counsel. Call your mentor or any godly woman who can offer you sound advice. Share the information you just read and ask for her feedback. Taking this action step will give you the wisdom you need to move forward or break things off.

Don't risk moving forward in a relationship with a guy who may have unaddressed sin issues. Don't minimize the red flags out of fear or worry. This is your one and only life. Think of your future. Think of the type of man you hope to spend the rest of your life with. Be willing to acknowledge the hard truth and seek outside help. Like we talked about in chapter 11, the more wisdom you can receive from wise outside individuals, the better equipped you will be to make a wise relationship decision.

Think of the type of man you hope to spend the rest of your life with.

As I (Bethany) shared at the beginning of this chapter, I am so grateful I heeded the red flags in my previous relationship. It saved me from moving forward into a potentially disastrous marriage. Don't make the mistake of ignoring the warning signs in your relationship. By taking them seriously now, you can avoid major regrets down the road.

CHAPTER 15

STUDY GUIDE

"Be honest with the reality of your relationship.
Don't ignore your concerns and expect them to go away.
Acknowledge the red flags for what they truly are."

1. Has there been a time in your life when you ignored an obvious red flag? What happened?

   _____

   _____

   _____

2. Why do you think it's easy to spot the red flags in your friends' relationships but harder to see them in your own?

   _____

   _____

   _____

3. Put an X next to any red flags that you've dealt with in the past or are currently facing:

   __He has a shallow relationship with God.

   __He pulls you down spiritually.

   __He's stuck in habitual sin.

   __He pressures you to compromise sexually.

   __He's rushing the relationship.

   __Wise people in your life don't support the relationship.

___ He has very few spiritual convictions.

___ He doesn't keep his word.

___ He wants to keep the relationship a secret.

___ He's obsessed with himself.

4. Why is it dangerous to minimize red flags in a relationship?

_____

_____

_____

MAKE IT *personal*

If you're in a relationship: Are there any red flags you need to acknowledge and seek outside counsel about? If so, take those concerns to a wise person who can offer you wisdom and advice.

If you're not in a relationship: Take some time to reread through each red flag so you'll be better prepared to spot them in any future relationships.

16. HOW DO I KNOW IF HE'S "THE ONE"?

I (Kristen) still remember that life-changing moment. The moment I knew, deep in my heart, that I was ready to spend the rest of my life with Zack. We weren't engaged yet but had been together for over eight months. By this point in our relationship, we had asked each other all the hard questions. We had sought endless counsel and outside input. We had eliminated all red flags. Our visions and passions were in alignment. Both of our families were on board and enthusiastic.

Zack and I were enjoying a lovely dinner together on the patio of a local restaurant in celebration of his twenty-second birthday. It was a warm May evening. As we chatted across the table from each other, memories and conversations from the past eight months flooded my mind. Our journey together had been an incredible time of growth and discovery. I felt a profound sense of love swell up in my heart for this handsome man. Zack's vision, passions, and purpose in life were something I truly valued and admired. He had proven to be a man of faithfulness, integrity, and humility. I had come to greatly respect him in every way.

Without saying a word, my heart made a silent confirmation. *I love him. I love him so much. He is the one I want to spend the rest of my life with.*

Is He "the One"?

"How did you know Zack was 'the one'?" one of my friends asked me recently.

This is the most common question I've been asked since marrying Zack. When I was a single woman, I remember asking myself that exact same question. "How will I know if he's the one? When will I know? Will it be obvious?" If you're single right now, you've probably wondered the exact same thing too.

I'll be the first to admit that many times early in my relationship with Zack I wished for a "magic" sign. Things would have been so much easier if a banner had dropped from the sky that read, "Zack will be your future husband!" But, alas, it didn't. Instead, I had to put my faith and trust in God.

Although this popular question seems mysterious and complex, it's really not. It's much simpler than we make it out to be. "How do I know if he's the one?" is a great question to ask. However, we need to be careful to approach this question in the right way, as it can actually lead to far more confusion than clarity if we approach it with the wrong motivation. Let's quickly break down two of the most popular wrong approaches when it comes to this question. Then we'll unpack the right approach.

WRONG APPROACH #1: HOW DO I KNOW IF HE'S THE ONE . . . FOR ME?

Asking the question, "How do I know if he's the one . . . for *me*?" seems harmless at first glance. And honestly, the two of us asked this question quite a bit during our previous relationships with Ryan and Justin. It wasn't until after our relationships ended that we realized the question's major flaws. Here's what we mean.

When we, as Christian women, ask the question in this way, we've instantly made the relationship all about us. We begin to view the guy through the lens of personal fulfillment. "Will he make *me* happy?" "Do I feel fulfilled when I'm with him?" "Does he complement me perfectly?" "Will he meet all my needs?" "Does he understand my every desire?" "Will he complete *me*?"

If you're constantly evaluating whether a guy is "the perfect fit for you," you'll measure all his qualifications from a lens of selfishness. His worthiness will be completely dependent on how he serves *you*. How he meets *your* needs. How he makes *you* feel. What he has to offer *you*. You will place yourself at the center of the relationship. You will be on a constant hunt for Mr. Perfectly-Fits-You-in-Every-Way. And if you do find a man who seems to meet all your needs, it will only be a matter of time before he sorely disappoints you. And if you end up marrying a man based on this motivation, you will most likely struggle down the road with doubts and fears whenever he fails to measure up.

WRONG APPROACH #2: HOW DO I KNOW IF HE'S . . . MY SOUL MATE?

As popular as that previous question is, another question is even more popular. "How do I know if he's . . . my soul mate?" is the number one question single women ask. "One Rutgers University study found that 94 percent of single women in their twenties say that the first requirement in a spouse is that he's a soul mate, someone with whom they feel an almost cosmic connection."[1] As sweet as this question sounds, it carries with it some major flaws.

"Our culture has widely embraced the notion that there is just one person who can . . . 'complete us.' This is a perilous mind-set with which to approach a lifelong marital decision, even though it is the majority opinion."[2]

First, the Bible has not made it clear to us whether God has ordained one specific soul mate for each of us. Yes, God is completely sovereign, but the way He brings couples together is truly a mystery. We cannot fully understand how God's sovereignty and man's responsibility work together here (see Deut. 29:29). Rather than trying to *find* our perfect soul mate, we need to make wise relationship decisions guided by the principles from God's Word.

Secondly, if you approach your love life with the soul mate perspective, you'll form the perfect dream man in your mind and then live your life on the hunt for that one man. For example, you walk into your Bible study class and there's a new guy visiting. *He could be my soul mate!* you think. Or maybe you're trying out a new restaurant and you discover that your cute waiter is a Christian. *Hmmmm . . . he could be my soul mate!* This approach puts you on a constant hunt for your perfect lifelong partner. You will be driven by your emotions and infatuation. You will be tempted to evaluate every guy on whether he "feels" like your soul mate rather than carefully and patiently getting to know his character and heart.

> Rather than trying to **find** our perfect soul mate, we need to make wise relationship decisions guided by the principles from God's Word.

This approach is often shortsighted, self-centered, and feelings-based in nature. Getting married becomes a desperate search to find your one needle in a haystack of seven billion people.

Sadly, women who have married men based on the soul mate approach have confessed to struggling with doubts later on in their marriages. If their husbands acted differently and didn't meet their needs like they used to, the wives would question whether they actually married their *true* soul mate. *Maybe he isn't my soul mate after all*, they fear. This reality is played out in modern chick flicks all the time. Wives are willing to ditch their covenant marriages to chase after their "true" soul mate.

RIGHT APPROACH: HOW DO I KNOW IF HE'S THE ONE . . . I WANT TO COMMIT MY LIFE TO?

Now that we've unpacked the two most popular wrong approaches for finding the one, let's unpack the right approach. The process for discovering if a man is the one is just that—a process. You won't know right away. In fact, you won't know until you've spent a good amount of time getting to know him. Instead of selfishly looking for someone to meet all your needs and fulfill your destiny, here's the right question to ask: "How do I know if he's the one . . . I want to commit my life to?"

Back in chapter 5, we talked about the fact that marriage and love shouldn't be built on feelings and emotions (alone). True agape love is built on a foundation of self-sacrifice. God-defined marriages are built on a foundation of lifelong commitment. When trying to discern whether a man is the one, you need to ask yourself if you are willing to love and be committed to this guy for the rest of your life. Since you're both imperfect sinners, you have to be willing to commit (for better or for worse) to selflessly loving this particular sinner until you die.

When approaching a relationship with commitment in mind, you will be much more careful to do the necessary legwork before saying, "I do." Knowing if a guy is the one you want to commit your life to will only become clear after spending quality time together. You will need to ask all the hard questions. You will need to see each other's true colors. You'll have to work through disagreements. Eliminate red flags. Seek outside counsel. Pray a lot separately and together. And you'll need to share the same vision, passion, and purpose. Only then will you be able to truly know if you want to commit your entire life to this guy. And if you are willing to commit to him . . . guess what? You've probably found the one.

Finding the one isn't a mysterious search; it's a practical and exciting adventure built on wisdom, prayer, counsel, commitment, and sacrificial love.

For Better or for Worse

When I sat at that dinner table across from Zack, I knew in my heart that he was the man I wanted to commit my life to. I knew because we had both put the time and effort into getting to know each other. I knew this man's heart. I knew his passions. I saw his love for God. I trusted him. I respected him. And because of all these things and more, I knew he was the one.

Zack was the man I wanted to serve the Lord with. He was the man I wanted to grow old with. He was the man I wanted to put the gospel on display with. He was the man I wanted to commit my life to. And a few short months after this dinner, Zack got down on one knee and asked me to be his one.

Fast-forward to our wedding day.

When Zack and I stood across from each other at the altar and shared our wedding vows, we were committing (before God) to be each other's ones from that moment forward. When we both said, "I do," we entered into a lifelong covenant before our families, friends, and most importantly, God. Never again would we have to wonder who the one was. We now knew. It was official. For better or for worse. And now it was our job to be faithful to the covenant. "What therefore God has joined together, let not man separate" (Mark 10:9).

Contrary to Hollywood's shallow messages about true love, marriage isn't so much about fireworks and perfect matches as it is about lasting, sacrificial commitment. It's about selflessly agreeing

> *Marriage isn't so much about fireworks and perfect matches as it is about lasting, sacrificial commitment.*

to love another human until you die. It's about choosing to join lives as a team to serve and glorify God together.

Once you stand at the altar with your man and say, "I do," you've found your permanent one. From that point forward, no matter what happens, that man will always be the one for you. He is the one you have entered into a covenant with. He is the one you've committed your life to. He is the one you must choose to stay faithful to until you die.

In our modern day and age, words like *faithfulness*, *lifelong commitment*, and *covenant* are not very popular. Instead, we prefer words such as *soul mate*, *true love*, and *happiness*. But the truth is, these feelings-based words do not produce the type of enduring marriages that we long for. If you desire to marry a man "until death do you part," you must marry someone who is committed to God's version of covenant-keeping love. This type of love stays faithful no matter what. This type of love gives when little is given back. This type of love fights when the other is giving up. Just as Christ loves his bride (the Church) unconditionally, we must marry with that same covenant-keeping love in mind. As John Piper says so well, "Marriage is designed to be a unique display of God's covenant grace because, unlike all other human relationships, the husband and wife are bound by covenant into the closest possible relationship for a lifetime."[3]

God will give you the wisdom to navigate through this exciting process.

If you're currently thinking, *Wow, this whole lifelong commitment thing is kind of serious and extreme*, then you're on the right track. Marriage is serious. Commitment is extreme. Covenant is permanent. Choosing a partner is a weighty decision. It shouldn't be taken lightly or casually.

However, getting married doesn't need to scare you. (Breathe deeply.) If you surround your relationship with outside wisdom, prayer, counsel, and good questions, you don't need to fear. God will give you the wisdom to navigate this exciting process.

Ask Good Questions

If you're in a relationship right now with a guy and you're trying to figure out if he's the one, the best thing you can do is work through some in-depth questions (assuming you've already sought outside counsel, eliminated red flags, etc.). Take a moment to slowly work through each of the following questions.

- HAVE I PRAYED DILIGENTLY ABOUT MARRYING THIS GUY?
- HAVE I BEEN IN THE WORD, SEEKING GOD'S TRUTH?
- DO I WANT TO SPEND THE REST OF MY LIFE WITH THIS GUY?
- CAN I SEE MYSELF GROWING OLD WITH HIM?
- AM I EXCITED ABOUT THE IDEA OF HIM BEING A FATHER TO MY CHILDREN?
- DO I HAVE ANY ADDITIONAL CONCERNS BEFORE MOVING FORWARD?
- HAVE I SOUGHT AND LISTENED TO WISE COUNSEL?
- DO I HAVE GENUINE JOY AND EXCITEMENT ABOUT MOVING FORWARD?
- DO I HAVE ANY SECRET RESERVATIONS ABOUT GETTING MARRIED TO THIS GUY?
- AM I WILLING TO LOVE AND SERVE THIS GUY FOR THE REST OF MY LIFE?
- IS HE WILLING TO LOVE AND SERVE ME FOR THE REST OF HIS LIFE?
- AM I SPIRITUALLY MATURE AND READY TO TAKE ON A LIFE-LONG COMMITMENT?
- WOULD GOD BE HONORED BY THIS MARRIAGE?

Sometimes all it takes are a few good questions to reveal whether you're ready to commit your life to a certain man.

I (Bethany) used these exact same questions not too long ago myself. I was in a relationship with a really godly man. However, the more I got to know him, the more I couldn't see myself spending the rest of my life with him. I honestly wasn't excited about the idea of growing old with him. I didn't have genuine joy about moving forward. There weren't any major red flags or problems; I just couldn't see myself actually marrying him.

Those helpful questions revealed to me that this man wasn't the one I wanted to commit my life to. And so, with graciousness and Christlike love, I broke things off.

As you reach a more serious stage in your relationship, be diligent to ask yourself these same valuable questions. They will help you determine whether you're willing and/or ready to commit your life to this one man.

Beyond the Wedding Day

As I (Kristen) think back to my wedding day, I smile at how beautiful and memorable it was. But as wonderful as my wedding day was, the actual marriage has been so much more incredible. I wake up every morning next to a man who genuinely loves God with his entire heart. He sacrifices for me every day. He works hard and loves others well. He joyfully serves in our local church. He prays with me every morning and evening.

Marrying a man of godly character has been, by far, one of the greatest blessings in my entire life. Our marriage hasn't been without some serious challenges and trials (multiple miscarriages, unexplained infertility, our own personal sin struggles, and more), but those challenges have only pushed us closer to Christ—and to each other. Our infatuation has grown into a deep-rooted, enduring, wholehearted kind of love. Zack and I are both just as committed to each other now as the day we got married.

As wonderful (and sanctifying) as our marriage has been, it's actually not the most important thing to Zack or me. Oh, we *love* being married—but we love Someone else even more. We love the Creator of marriage Himself. God is the most important thing in this world to us. Marriage has never satisfied either of us the way our relationship with God has. Nothing is more precious than our Savior. But the beautiful thing is, the more we love Jesus, the more we value and love each other. The more we focus on Christ, the more our marriage thrives.

The more we focus on Christ, the more our marriage thrives.

As you ask yourself the question, "How do I know if he's the one I want to commit my life to?" choose to keep Christ at the center of your heart and mind. Choose to seek God first (see Matt. 6:33). Always put your hope in God above anything else. Find your full satisfaction in Christ alone. Before you commit your heart to one man, make sure your heart is fully devoted to the Man. By keeping Christ at the center of your heart and wisely marrying a man of godly character, you will lay a strong foundation for glorifying God in your marriage.

CHAPTER 16

STUDY GUIDE

"Finding the one isn't a mysterious search;
it's a practical and exciting adventure built on wisdom,
prayer, counsel, commitment, and sacrificial love."

1. How did Zack and Kristen's story help you clarify the question, "How do you know if he's the one?"

   _____

   _____

   _____

2. In the wrong approach #2, we asked the question, "How do I know if he's . . . my soul mate?" Although this is a popular question to ask, why do you think it's not the most helpful approach?

   _____

   _____

   _____

3. How is the right approach—"How do I know if he's the one . . . I want to commit my life to?"—different from the other two approaches?

   _____

   _____

   _____

4. "What therefore God has joined together, let not man separate" (Mark 10:9). How should this verse impact your view of marriage and commitment?

_____

_____

_____

5. As wonderful as marriage is, why is it *not* the most important thing?

_____

_____

_____

MAKE IT *personal*

If you had to be totally honest, which would you say is the most important thing in your life—getting married or your relationship with Christ? How can you strive to build a closer relationship with Christ starting today?

PART FIVE

Living Well on This Side of the Altar

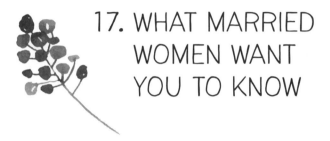

17. WHAT MARRIED WOMEN WANT YOU TO KNOW

We, Kristen and Bethany, were on a weekend camping trip with some family and friends when we made a stupid decision. It all started when one of our friends walked over and asked, "Hey, are y'all up for an adventure?" Without hesitation, our teenage selves quickly responded yes!

Without telling our parents, the two of us, along with two of our friends, snuck off for an adventure.

"Okay," one of our friends said mischievously as we accelerated down a country road. "Have y'all ever been cow tipping?" Our eyes widened with excited curiosity.

"Nooo," Bethany said with raised eyebrows, "but we've always wanted to try it. Let's do it!"

Within a few minutes we came upon some large fields filled with cows. Our friend slowed down the truck and turned off the headlights. We didn't want to wake any slumbering beasts. Never mind the diesel engine roaring as we pulled up. We turned into a grassy shoulder next to the dirt road. A quick scan confirmed that nobody else was here. We quietly got out of the truck and tiptoed through the tall grass toward the barbed wire fence. Did we mention we were in Texas, where everyone owns guns? Oh, and did we mention we were about to trespass on someone's private property? Yeah. Stupid decision number one.

As we snuck through the barbed wire fence, the four of us decided to turn off our cell phones completely. We didn't want to accidentally wake the cows. Oh, and we didn't want our parents to be able to reach us either. We weren't interested in letting them know what we were doing. Stupid decision number two.

With a full moon rising above us, we cautiously waded through a sea of cacti and weeds. Once we were within twenty feet of the herd, one of our friends initiated a huddle to formulate a game plan. We agreed to work as a team to tip one cow. Our strategy was simple. Sneak up to the sleeping cow and push it over on the count of three. Did we mention we were all wearing bright white shirts too? Yeah. And it didn't help that the full moon illuminated our every move. Stupid decision number three.

As our friends led the way, we followed close behind. Once we were within six feet of a cow, we froze. Cows are *a lot* bigger in person than they look from the highway. They're huge animals capable of doing some serious damage if they charge. Suddenly, out of nowhere, a huge bull emerged from the darkness. This was the daddy of all bulls. And he wasn't happy that we were messing with his females.

> *Cows are **a lot** bigger in person than they look from the highway.*

"Run!" one of our friends suddenly shouted. Without hesitation, the four of us bolted for the fence. With our hearts pounding and sweat dripping down our faces, we quickly and cautiously squeezed back through the barbed wire fence. Once we were back inside the truck, we all burst into nervous laughter. As we headed back toward the campground, we knew we were in for it.

Let's just say that wasn't one of our wisest moments. The minute our parents saw us walk into the campground, the questions began. We eventually confessed the whole story. They were extremely disappointed in our lack of judgment, to say the least. Not to mention our deliberate act of turning off all forms of communication. Yeah. We definitely got in trouble. Also, a farmer could have shot us for trespassing. Or a bull could have trampled us. Or the police could have caught us for breaking the law. Not smart.

Looking back now, the two of us laugh at that story and wonder what in the world we were thinking. If only we could go back in time and give our younger teen selves some advice. Unfortunately, we had to learn some things the hard way.

Been There, Done That

Most of us have made stupid decisions in our pasts. We all have done things we wish we could get a do-over on, right? Being older now, we see things more clearly. We have more wisdom. More discretion. More experience. There's something to be said about growing older and learning from life's many past mistakes. There is wisdom in age.

We need to take advantage of the wisdom of women who are older than we are.

Since none of us can go back in time, we need to take advantage of the next best thing—learning from those who have gone before us. We need to take advantage of the wisdom of women who are older than we are. Those who have experienced far more than we have. Older women can't go back in time, but they can teach us what they wish they had done differently. They can help us avoid some of the mistakes they have made. This is what mentoring and discipleship is all about.

In fact, God Himself is such a fan of older women teaching younger women that he actually commands it in Titus 2:3–4.

"Older women likewise are to be reverent in behavior, not slanderers or slaves to much wine. They are to teach what is good, and so train the young women to love their husbands and children."

That you're reading this book means you probably desire to have a godly marriage and home one day. If that is the case, you need to be intentional to learn from older Christian women who can teach you how to do that.

The two of us have been greatly impacted by the older women who have poured into our lives. We want you to experience that same benefit. With that being said, we have something special for you. In this chapter, we are bringing four older godly women right to *you*. These four women have been married for thirty, forty, and fifty-plus years, and they love the Lord deeply. They know what it takes to build a strong marriage and family. And they want to help you get off to a great start. These women want to teach you how to prepare for marriage, starting now. They want to teach you what they wish they'd known years ago. They want to help you build a strong foundation that will bless your future husband and family.

We've asked each of these women different questions. Their candid advice is invaluable. So sit back, relax, grab a delicious cup of coffee, and enjoy the incredible (and sometimes hilarious) insights you're about to receive.

YVONNE WELCH (MARRIED SINCE 1966)

How can I, as a single woman, best prepare to be a helper to my future husband?

Many times a young bride will look to her new husband to satisfy all the deepest desires of her heart. She will expect him to do what only God can do—give her total joy and fulfillment. In her book *Loneliness*, Elisabeth Elliot says, "One of the surprises in store for most brides and grooms is that they are still lonely. A common but unreasonable expectation about marriage, and there are many unreasonable ones, is that the partner will now fill the place of everybody on whom one depended before, father, mother, brothers, sisters, and friends. Because falling in love is an all consuming, preoccupied, and exclusive phenomena, it can be very hard on other relationships that no longer seem to be needed. But marriage teaches us that even the most intimate human companionship cannot satisfy the deepest places of the heart. Our hearts are lonely till they rest in Him who made us for himself. Having been married to three very different men [separated by death], all of them fine Christian husbands, I have found that not one of them, or even all three of them together if I had been a polyandrist, could meet all my needs. The Bible promises that my God, not my husband, shall supply all my needs."[1]

If a wife continues to depend on her husband instead of on Jesus Christ, she may easily become the contentious woman from Proverbs 27:15. When you, as a single woman, learn to take all your cares, fears, and concerns to the Lord Jesus Christ on a daily basis, your heart will be strengthened. You will be preparing yourself to be a godly helpmate to your future husband.

Personally, I love to invest time with the Lord early in the morning so that I will be strengthened for the challenges of the day. God uses this to encourage my heart and comfort me. This habit has been the means God has used in my life as a channel of His grace to fortify me for the challenges of life. I believe this could be the greatest preparation that you, as a single woman, could make to equip yourself to be an encourager and helper to your future husband.

> When you, as a single woman, learn to take all your cares, fears, and concerns to the Lord Jesus Christ on a daily basis, your heart will be strengthened.

221

What caught you by surprise during your first year of marriage?

The first surprise, or rather shock, came when we had only been married a few days. We had just returned from our honeymoon, and I had taken all our clothes to the laundromat. I left the clothes in the washing machine and went shopping. When I returned to get our clothes, someone had stolen them! I drove back to our apartment and excitedly exclaimed, "Bob, guess what! Someone has stolen all our clothes, but don't worry. You and I can go shopping and charge all new clothes."

He immediately said, "I don't believe in charge accounts."

I was shocked. How could you live without a charge card?

He then said, "I think we should pray for some new clothes or some incredible bargain that fits our budget."

I had prayed for a godly man but had assumed he would be one that fit in a little better with my financial policy. The Lord had to really help me get over that surprise, and I began looking for some incredible bargains.

KIMBERLY WAGNER (MARRIED SINCE 1981)

What is one character quality you would encourage me, as a single woman, to start developing now in preparation for my future marriage?

It wasn't until we reached a critical state in our marriage that I realized the power of a simple thing like appreciation. Appreciation is an action, not just a character quality, we need to cultivate. There is an art to demonstrating it. Appreciation goes beyond gratitude; it communicates value—not only gratitude for what someone can do for you, but appreciation for who they are and for the potential of who they can become.

Demonstrating appreciation (appropriately) to the men in your life now, as a single woman, will develop a heart that serves to help others be all God created them to be. We are designed as an essential strengthening counterpart (see Gen. 2:18). Whether you're single or married, you're designed to come alongside others and strengthen their efforts by being a type of "life-giver." Appreciation does that; it breathes life into those we serve. Even a small thank-you for something as simple as taking out the trash encourages a man. Gratitude, expressed in creative and thoughtful ways, conveys appreciation, and most husbands thrive from it.

Appreciation from a wife has the potential to inspire her man to become the leader God created him to be. Men are wired to be courageous leaders, but far too many husbands end up retreating to a cave of passivity rather than boldly moving ahead into the unknown. I speak from experience; my husband stayed in his cave for several years. If a man is questioned over every decision he makes, criticized rather than affirmed, and treated like a child, typically that man will step away from the leadership role and let his wife take the wheel. When that happens, you have a mess on your hands.

> *Appreciation from a wife has the potential to inspire her man to become the leader God created him to be.*

As a single woman, you have a tremendous power of influence as you encourage your friend, coworker, brother, or future husband to accomplish a specific task by demonstrating appreciation for what they are attempting.

If you read through the pages of my journal, you would find that I often inscribe these words as an initiative for my day: "My objective today is to encourage and infuse strength into my man." Knowing we are both involved in a spiritual battle that we cannot see, I expect attacks to come, temptations to hit, and I prepare myself beforehand. Before I'm tempted to grumble, complain, or vent my emotions, I need to stabilize my heart with the objective of demonstrating life-giving appreciation to my husband through-out the day.

What caught you by surprise during your first year of marriage?

This sounds naive, but I thought husbands and wives had phys-ical intimacy (not sure the appropriate words to use here, but I think you get the picture) *every single* night. I mean, that's what a mar-riage bed is made for, right? And you'd rather do that than sleep, right? I was wrong. On the third night of our honeymoon, LeRoy was too tuckered out to do more than barely kiss me goodnight before he was snoring. And my heart was broken. I was devastated. I immediately thought, *He doesn't love me. He doesn't enjoy me. He'd rather sleep than make love to me.* Which, on some days, is true—he would rather sleep, but only because he's flat-out exhausted, not because he doesn't enjoy our intimacy or doesn't love me.

HEIDI BAIRD (MARRIED SINCE 1982)

What are some practical ways I can build a strong relationship with God now, as a single woman?

The other day, my youngest daughter, Sue, encouraged me to take one of those personality tests. To nobody's surprise, I scored 99.9 percent extrovert. Yes, I'm one of those very annoying people who wakes up like it's Christmas every day.

I have always been excited about life and adventures, but un-fortunately, as a young single girl, life was more about me than God. At seventeen, this 99.9 percent extrovert would wake up to have a devotional time with God each morning but was having trouble being still for more than five minutes. I found my mind drifting off to my plans for the day or a recent conversation I had with my boyfriend. I was so distracted and couldn't seem to force myself to stay focused on my quiet time. I'd apologize to God for my distracted mind about twenty times and then start over.

Nothing changed until my wise mentor, Mrs. Walker, asked me an eye-opening question. "Heidi," she said gently, "how can you have an intimate relationship with someone you don't even know?"

Ouch. But she was right. I didn't really *know* God. Sadly, He felt far away and boring to me. I had no problem spending time with my boyfriend. I was interested in his thoughts, and it was fun to be with him. We could talk for hours and my mind didn't drift off. I wanted to learn how to love God like that.

Thankfully, Mrs. Walker helped me learn how to do just that. Here are three life-changing habits Mrs. Walker encouraged me to put into practice as a young woman:

1. I WOULD GET UP EARLY EACH MORNING WITH MY BIBLE AND A NOTEPAD IN HAND, THEN GO SIT IN MY CLOSET (A LESS DISTRACTING PLACE) AND WRITE OUT AS MANY CHARACTER QUALITIES THAT I KNEW ABOUT GOD. (GOD IS PATIENT, GOD IS FORGIVING, GOD IS HOLY, ETC.)

2. NEXT, I WOULD PRAY AND ASK GOD TO HELP ME KNOW HIM MORE DEEPLY AND MORE INTIMATELY. ("DRAW NEAR TO GOD AND HE WILL DRAW NEAR TO YOU," JAMES 4:8 NKJV.)

3. FINALLY, I WOULD TAKE ONE OF GOD'S CHARACTER QUALITIES FROM MY LIST AND LOOK UP A FEW VERSES THAT GAVE ME BETTER INSIGHT INTO THAT PARTICULAR QUALITY. THEN I WOULD MEDITATE ON ONE OR TWO OF THOSE VERSES ALL DAY.

After several weeks of doing this, being in my closet became exciting for me! For the first time in my life I was experiencing the amazing, awesome, and intimate relationship with my Father that I had longed for.

If you're not sure how to build a deep relationship with God, I encourage you to do what Mrs. Walker encouraged me to do those many years ago. Grab your Bible, a notebook, and a pen, and settle into a quiet spot (closets are my go-to choice) to begin writing out as many character qualities of God that come to your mind. Then meditate on one of those a day. Look up verses that teach you more. Spend time thanking God for who He is.

I encourage you to do this for the next few weeks each morning. Like I did, I bet you'll see a transformation in your quiet time and love for the Lord.

What caught you by surprise during your first year of marriage?

After my husband and I returned home from our honeymoon trip and were settling into our new life together, I discovered that he liked to be in bed at 9:00 p.m. For this night owl who normally went to bed after midnight, this shocked me. I loved late-night, intimate, heartfelt talks. So, like any newly married couple, we compromised. I would go to bed early with him, but then he would stay awake long enough to have some heartfelt conversations with me. That seemed fair.

This was working well until one night, when I was in the middle of sharing my deepest, most heartfelt thoughts, and I looked over to see my husband's eyes closed! He was sleeping. Like sound asleep and snoring. *What? How could he?* I soon began to learn that my sweet husband only had about fifteen minutes of listening in him at bedtime. I concluded that I would just have to learn to talk faster.

 ## BARBARA RAINEY (MARRIED SINCE 1972)

What practical homemaking skills would be helpful for me, as a single woman, to develop?

When my children were all five and under, we were friends with a very energetic widow in our small church. One day after we'd been to her house, my young son said to me, "Mommy, I like going to Miss Kitty's house." "Why?" I asked. "Because it's so warm," he replied, candidly.

I knew he didn't mean temperature but something else more intangible. My immediate thought was, *Does my home feel warm to those who visit us?* My little Benjamin felt this single woman's warm welcome, her kind acceptance of rambunctious kids, her engaging interest in our family, her heart of kindness and love for anyone who crossed her threshold.

Homemaking is the art of making a house a home.

Homemaking is the art of making a house a home. It is not the exclusive domain of married women who have a house full of wedding gifts with which to serve and entertain others. It is not dependent on fully developed cooking or decorating talents.

A house becomes a home first of all when humans enter to live there. But as my little son understood, it's not just a place inhabited by people. My single daughter's first home was a newly remodeled little bungalow previously inhabited by a drug-addicted young man and his dog. No one would describe that structure as a warm home.

So as you enjoy these years as a single woman, and I pray you will, use your apartment, rented bungalow, or shared house to invite friends and family in for meals, Bible studies, and holiday celebrations.

But most importantly, may I encourage you to learn the number one homemaking skill? That skill is surrendering your heart to Jesus every single day. Our friend, Miss Kitty, lived a life surrendered to Jesus. It was His presence in her that greeted us every time we went to her house.

Cooking and decorating classes abound. You can take one or more anytime, anywhere. But creating a warm home that even little children recognize is possible only when your heart is completely His.

What caught you by surprise during your first year of marriage?

Honestly, many things surprised me during the first year, but one of the first was how differently we viewed the spending of our very limited combined incomes. I was shocked that he thought it was perfectly fine to buy more fishing gear when we had our books and many other things stored on boards between stacked concrete cinder blocks! The fact that he thought our temporary solution to no furniture was perfectly fine and good enough to last for months or years made my head hurt from bewilderment.

It was a clash of values. It was also the beginning of decades of merging our values through endless conversations to understand why his hobbies were important to him and why having storage was important to me.

Keep Learning, Girl

The two of us hope the wisdom, advice, and counsel from these four godly women blessed your socks off as much as it did ours. We hope you were challenged and inspired by what these women shared. We, as younger women, can learn so much from the older women in our lives. God's plan in Titus 2 is truly brilliant.

Choose to tap into the endless wisdom and counsel available to you from the godly women in your life.

Don't try to figure out everything about singleness, romance, relationships, and marriage on your own. Choose to tap into the endless wisdom and counsel available to you from the godly women in your life. Reach out to them and ask them to share their insights with you. Start by asking them the same questions Yvonne, Kim, Heidi, and Barbara were asked. Then come up with some additional ones on your own. If you don't personally know any godly women, be intentional to get your hands on some resources written by godly women. For starters, Kim Wagner and Barbara Rainey both have wonderful published resources that you can find online and in stores. Don't bypass this incredible and priceless opportunity. You will be amazed by how much there truly is to learn.

CHAPTER 17

STUDY GUIDE

"Don't try to figure out everything about singleness, romance, relationships, and marriage on your own. Choose to tap into the endless wisdom and counsel available to you from the godly women in your life."

1. Describe a time in your life when you made a poor decision based on a lack of maturity (e.g., cow tipping).

   _____

   _____

   _____

2. Circle all the things older women are called to teach younger women in Titus 2:3–4. "Older women likewise are to be reverent in behavior, not slanderers or slaves to much wine. They are to teach what is good, and so train the young women to love their husbands and children."

   _____

   _____

   _____

   What value do you see in learning from older women?

   _____

   _____

   _____

3. What was your greatest takeaway from the advice of each woman?

Yvonne Welch: _____

_____

_____

_____

Kimberly Wagner: _____

_____

_____

_____

Heidi Baird: _____

_____

_____

_____

Barbara Rainey: _____

_____

_____

_____

4. List two ways that your life would specifically benefit from having a mentor.

_____

_____

MAKE IT *personal*

Is there an older woman in your community who could be a Titus 2 woman in your life by mentoring you? Seriously consider reaching out to her for mentorship.

18. A LOVE STORY WORTH FIGHTING FOR

It was a warm summer evening and the two of us were getting ready to head out on the town for a fun sister dinner date. With Kristen getting married to Zack in just a few short weeks, we wanted to enjoy our final moments of being "single sisters" together. We both knew that our lives were about to change in a really big (but really exciting) way.

As we pulled out of the driveway and headed down the street, the two of us started reminiscing about some of our favorite sister memories. We talked about everything from our past crushes to our crazy cow-tipping adventure to Kristen's hilariously embarrassing NASCAR driving incident to Bethany's shoe-throwing scandal.

The more we talked, the more we noticed a trending theme in our conversation. The topics of guys, love, and romance were a big part of our pasts. Although it was easy to look back on the memories and laugh now, we both knew the reality of how hard it had been. We both clearly remembered how challenging those teenage years were. Striving after purity and trying to embrace God's design for love hadn't been a walk in the park. There were times of wondering if God's ways truly were best. There were times of feeling alone and lonely in our pursuit of God's design for purity. And there were times of questioning if guys with vision, passion, and purpose still existed (thankfully, Zack showed us they did).

> *Despite our challenges and questions, we both truly believed God's ways were worth fighting for.*

Despite our challenges and questions, we both truly believed God's ways were worth fighting for. As time went on, we began to experience the blessing and joy of living for His glory, and we were confident that it was worth it. With Kristen's wedding just around the corner, we'd seen firsthand the beauty of pursuing a relationship according to God's good design. We'd seen the benefits of embracing purity. We'd seen the joy that comes from centering a relationship on Christ and making His glory the focus.

And even though I (Bethany) was single at the time (and still am), I was confident that God's ways were better. I was convinced that doing relationships according to God's design was the best way to go. Watching Kristen joyfully approach her wedding day reassured me that embracing love defined by God was worth the pursuit.

Fighting for Love Defined by God

Let's be real for a minute. Embracing God's design for true love isn't easy. It's completely countercultural. What the two of us have written in this book takes a whole lot of guts, gumption, grace, and prayer to live out. Thankfully, with Christ's strength, we can be victorious.

> THE LORD IS MY STRENGTH AND MY SHIELD; IN HIM MY HEART TRUSTS, AND I AM HELPED; MY HEART EXULTS, AND WITH MY SONG I GIVE THANKS TO HIM. THE LORD IS THE STRENGTH OF HIS PEOPLE. (PS. 28:7-8)

When it comes to God's design for love, the two of us have often felt like lone fish in a big ocean. It seems as though most people are swimming in one direction and we're swimming in the other. In moments like these, it can be hard to stay the course, to swim against the flow. To help us stay on track, we've needed regular reminders of God's bigger picture. We've needed reminders of *why* we embrace God's design for love, marriage, and sex. We've needed reminders of *Whose* glory we're truly living for. The more we've focused on God's truth, the easier it has become to stand strong.

We encourage you to do the same thing. As you embrace God's design, you may often feel as though you're the only one pursuing it. At times everyone may be swimming against God's truth, and you'll have to make the tough choice to swim in the opposite direction. Even if everyone around you is ditching purity, God will give you the strength to stand strong. Even if all your friends are having sex before marriage, you will know the value of saving it for marriage. Even if the women around you are marrying nonbelievers, you will understand the importance of waiting for a Christian man.

The more we've focused on God's truth, the easier it has become to stand strong.

Galatians 6:8–9 reminds us of the bigger picture. "For the one who sows to his own flesh will from the flesh reap corruption, but the one who sows to the Spirit will from the Spirit reap eternal life. And let us not grow weary of doing good, for in due season we will reap, if we do not give up." Focusing on God's bigger picture will help you stand strong and swim against the culture flow. And for the times that sin and failure do occur, remember that you have a heavenly Father who loves and cares for you deeply. His grace is sufficient for your every weakness. His forgiveness is available to those who confess their sins (see 1 John 1:9). May the words of Psalm 86:5 be a constant source of encouragement to you, as it is to us. "For you, O Lord, are good and forgiving, abounding in steadfast love to all who call upon you."

Love Defined Challenge

Throughout this book, you've learned some incredible truths. You've gained the knowledge of what love defined by God looks like. However, knowledge alone isn't enough. If you don't choose to put His truths into action, your life won't be changed. Your relationships won't look any different. Your love life won't be built on God's timeless design.

We want personally to challenge you to put the truths of this book into action. If you're ready to embrace God's spectacular design, we hope you'll take this Love Defined Challenge. Read through the following challenge and check off all the boxes of the things to which you're committed.

Trusting God with Your Love Story

I (Bethany) always dreamed of getting married young, but God obviously has different plans for my life. With no prospects on the horizon I'm continuing to trust God in this area. I'm striving to faithfully serve God right where He has me. I (Kristen) had always dreamed of having a house full of kids shortly after marriage. But even to this day there are no kids in sight. God clearly has a very different plan for my life. If there's one thing the two of us have learned, it's this: God's plans are often different from our plans. As Proverbs 16:9 says, "The heart of man plans his way, but the Lord establishes his steps."

Whether you're still in your teen years, your twenties, or well past them, the Lord will establish *His* good plan in your life. Regardless of how your future unfolds, you can still trust God's plan.

LOVE DEFINED CHALLENGE

I am committed to becoming a woman who strives to:

☐ Courageously reject the lies of the Fairy Tale Facade and instead looks to God's Word for truth.

☐ Boldly jump off the merry-go-round and instead pursues love according to God's Timeless Method for Lasting Relationships.

☐ Fully embrace God's spectacular design for love, marriage, and sex.

☐ Intentionally live out biblical femininity in my romantic relationships.

☐ Build God-honoring friendships with the guys in my life.

☐ Pursue romantic relationships with intentionality, prayer, outside wisdom, and accountability.

☐ Build my romantic relationships on a foundation of purity and holiness.

☐ Choose to T.R.U.S.T. God in my singleness.

☐ Take active steps to thrive as a single woman and serve those around me.

☐ Seek counsel and wisdom from older godly women to continue learning more about love defined by God.

We pray you will join us in bravely living out the Love Defined Challenge. You're not alone in this fight. Come link arms with thousands of other women who are striving for the same things. You can find amazing support through our online sisterhood over at GirlDefined.com.

If marriage is part of God's plan for your future at some point, then you can rest assured that His timing is perfect. You can leave the details of your story to Him. Whether you're single for a short season, a long season, or for your entire life, your calling doesn't change. Your job is to trust God and serve Him faithfully. Right now. Right where He has you.

As you trust God with your life and your future, we want to leave you with a powerful prayer of surrender, hope, and trust. This prayer has been a regular theme in our own lives. We encourage you to make it your own.

> *Dear heavenly Father,*
>
> *Thank You for teaching me about Your incredible design for love, relationships, and marriage. I am so grateful for Your Word and the wisdom it provides in my life. Please give me the courage to embrace and live out Your plan for Christ-centered love. Help me to honor and glorify You in my romantic relationships. Help me to trust You during seasons of singleness. Please give me the strength to wait patiently on Your good timing in my life. You are a good Father. I surrender my plans and dreams to You. Thank You for loving me so faithfully. May my life be an offering of praise and worship back to You. Amen.*

The two of us are cheering you on! Choosing to embrace God's plan for love isn't easy, but it is undoubtedly worth it. You will never regret choosing to do things God's way.

May you never grow weary of swimming against the cultural flow. May you never grow tired of glorifying God in your romantic relationships. May you never lose sight of chasing hard after purity. May you never stop growing in your understanding of Christ-centered love. As you embrace God's beautiful design for true love, romance, and lasting relationships, may your life be a beacon of hope in our lost and broken world. May the beauty of Christ's love shine through you as you courageously pursue love defined by God.

CHAPTER 18

STUDY GUIDE

"Choosing to embrace God's plan for love isn't easy, but it is undoubtedly worth it. You will never regret choosing to do things God's way."

1. How has this book most impacted your view of love and romance?

   _____

   _____

   _____

2. How will your future relationships be changed as a result of reading this book?

   _____

   _____

   _____

3. In what ways has your understanding of God grown as you've learned more about His bigger picture for love, marriage, and sex?

   _____

   _____

   _____

   _____

4. Embracing love defined by God won't be easy. How does Psalm 28:7–8 encourage you in this? "The LORD is my strength and my shield; in him my heart trusts, and I am helped; my heart exults, and with my song I give thanks to him. The LORD is the strength of his people."

_____

_____

_____

_____

5. If you have benefited from the wisdom in this book, don't keep it to yourself. Can you think of one friend who would benefit from the message of love defined by God? If so, we challenge you to do one of the following:

- get her a copy of this book and explain how it has inspired you or
- invite her to read it alongside you and discuss the book together.

MAKE IT *personal*

Are you committed to becoming a woman who embraces the ten points from the Love Defined Challenge? If so, we invite you to join us by signing your name below.

_____

Appendix A

FINDING FREEDOM AND FORGIVENESS FROM PAST SEXUAL SIN

Past sexual sin can feel profoundly weighty at times. It can feel overwhelming. Even all-consuming. When sexual sin is not dealt with in a biblical way, it will often bleed into the very fibers of how we view our identity. Undealt-with sin has a way of deceiving us into believing we are now worthless. Beyond forgiveness. Utterly ruined. But this is not true.

The two of us want you to know you are loved and valued by your Creator, regardless of your past. Yes, God is greatly grieved by our sin and calls us to repentance, but that does not change His ultimate love for us. Your worth is not defined by what you've done or by what's been done to you. Your worth is defined by God alone. And because of Him, you have immeasurable value. You have intrinsic importance because you are made in God's very image (see Gen. 1:26). Even when you were a tiny baby inside your mother's womb, God was there, handcrafting your existence into reality (see Ps. 139:13–15).

A simple illustration of our unchanging worth and value in God's eyes can be found in a one hundred–dollar bill. Imagine that you're holding a one hundred–dollar bill in your hand. Someone walks up to you and asks, "How much is that bill worth?" A little confused, you reply, "It's worth one hundred dollars." The person then proceeds to take the bill from your hand and crumbles it up in their own hands. Once the bill is nicely wrinkled, they drop it on the floor and stomp on it, grinding it into the ground. Next, they crumble it up even more in their sweaty hands. They then hand the crumbled, dirty, and slightly moist bill back to you. With some hesitation, you reach out and take it. "Open it up," they encourage you. You slowly unfold and uncrumple the weary-looking bill. Holding it up again, you notice that it looks different. It has a few black marks. It's covered with creases. It even has one small rip. "How much is it worth now?" the person asks you intently. Your eyes slowly lock onto theirs. After a few moments of thought, you say, "It's still worth one hundred dollars."

No amount of dirt or stains will change the value of a one hundred–dollar bill. We, as women, work the exact same way in God's eyes. Regardless of our past sexual sin or the sexual sins that have been committed against us, our worth remains the same. Sin may produce some creases, crumples, and tears in our lives, but it doesn't change our value.

If you have believed the lie that you are "less than" because of your past, don't believe it anymore. Put your hope and trust in the God who loves you and says you are precious to Him.

God's love for us is so incredibly mind-blowing because it is based not on anything we can do but solely on what Christ has done for us. "God shows his love for us in that while we were still sinners, Christ died for us" (Rom. 5:8). Jesus died because we're sinners, not because we're perfect Christian women. We need a Savior. We need the forgiveness and freedom that can only come through Jesus Christ. Galatians 5:1 exhorts us in this by saying,

"For freedom Christ has set us free; stand firm therefore, and do not submit again to a yoke of slavery." Christ died so we could be *freed* from our sin. We are no longer slaves. No matter how ugly, how dirty, or how shameful you feel about your past sexual sin, you can find freedom through Jesus Christ. And that can begin today. Right now.

Before reading the next section, take a moment to pause and pray. Spend a few minutes praising God for sending His Son, Jesus, to die on the cross for your sins (see John 3:16). Praise God for the value and worth that He alone has given you. Praise the name of Jesus for the power that He can give you to walk in freedom, truth, and light.

It's time to lay your burdens at the foot of the cross. We want to guide you through some practical steps for finding freedom. These are action steps that we see in Scripture for finding freedom from the bondage of sin. As you read each step, take a moment to pray and act on what is being said.

1. CONFESS YOUR PAST AND/OR CURRENT SEXUAL SIN TO GOD.

The very first step to finding freedom from sin is to humbly confess that sin to God. Pray and verbally confess to God that you have disobeyed His Word and have sinned against Him. Psalm 51 is an excellent section of Scripture to meditate on and pray through to help you confess sin. David penned this psalm after his sexual sin with Bathsheba. Allow the words of Psalm 51 to draw your heart back to God in repentance.

2. ACCEPT GOD'S FORGIVENESS.

Once you have confessed your sins, accept God's forgiveness. He promises to give you complete and total forgiveness. First John 1:9 says, "If we confess our sins, he is faithful and just to forgive us our sins and to cleanse us from all unrighteousness." God is faithful and will cleanse you from all unrighteousness if you confess. What a hopeful promise!

3. DIG BENEATH THE SURFACE.

Sexual sin is often the outworking of other sins (discontentment, lack of trust in God's plan, pride, ingratitude, rebellion, fear, etc.). Examine your heart and life and ask yourself, "Where did my heart go astray?"

Read the following list and see if any of these things were/are true in your life when the sexual sin took place:

- WAS I IN REBELLION?
- WAS MY RELATIONSHIP WITH GOD WEAK OR NONEXISTENT?
- DID I UNDERSTAND GOD'S INSTRUCTIONS REGARDING SEX?
- DID I GIVE IN TO PEER PRESSURE?
- DID I CHOOSE AN UNGODLY BOYFRIEND?
- WAS I IN A SECRET RELATIONSHIP?
- DID I FAIL TO SET UP MORAL BOUNDARIES?
- WAS I CONFUSED ABOUT THE TRUE MEANING OF LOVE?
- DID I COMPROMISE TO "FEEL" LIKE SOMEONE REALLY LOVED ME?
- DID ROMANCE NOVELS/MOVIES ENTICE ME TO BECOME SEXUALLY ACTIVE?

Did any of the above reasons contribute to your sexual sin? If so, be intentional to take action in that area. By digging a little deeper, you will be better equipped to attack the sin head-on and cut off those specific temptations.

4. ASK A GODLY WOMAN TO BE YOUR MENTOR.

Since we don't know the ins and outs of your personal struggles, we encourage you to connect with an older godly woman who can help you work through your struggles. Proactively pursue a relationship with this woman and ask her to mentor you. Be honest and open with her. Ask her for counsel and wisdom from God's Word.

5. FILL YOUR MIND WITH TRUTH.

The fact that you're reading this book is a sign that you desire to learn and grow in your understanding of God's design for love, marriage, and sex. Filling your mind with truth is essential as you move forward in faithfulness to God. In addition to reading this book, I highly encourage you to grab a copy of one or all of the following books:

Sex and the Single Girl (by Juli Slattery)

Meet Mr. Smith: Revolutionize the Way You Think about Sex, Purity, and Romance (by Eric and Leslie Ludy)

And the Bride Wore White: Seven Secrets to Sexual Purity (by Dannah Gresh)

Sex Is Not the Problem, Lust Is (by Joshua Harris)

Finally Free: Fighting for Purity with the Power of Grace (by Heath Lambert)

Freedom and forgiveness from sexual sin is available to you through the power and blood of our Savior, Jesus Christ. In Him, you have the ability to walk in the freedom and fullness that only He offers. May the beautiful words of Isaiah 61:3 wash over your heart and remind you that God is in the restoration business. "He will give a crown of beauty for ashes, a joyous blessing instead of mourning, festive praise instead of despair. In their righteousness, they will be like great oaks that the LORD has planted for his own glory" (NLT).

Appendix B

50 QUESTIONS TO ASK
EARLY IN THE RELATIONSHIP

GENERAL QUESTIONS TO ASK HIM

- Why do you want to be in a relationship with me?

- What do you see as my best character qualities?

- What do you see as my weakest character qualities?

- What does your vision of a happy family look like?

- What motivates and excites you?

- How would you describe a good work ethic?

- How important is integrity to you? Why?

- How would you maintain purity in our relationship?

- What are your personal views on alcohol?

- Have you ever had any seasons of rebellion in your life? If so, what happened?

- What are your views on politics?

- What does a typical week look like in your life?

SPIRITUAL QUESTIONS TO ASK HIM

- Can you explain the gospel to me?

- How important is your relationship with Jesus?

- What importance does prayer play in your life?

- What is your view on church involvement?

- What does your personal quiet time look like?

- How would you lead your family spiritually?

- What is your perspective on sharing the gospel?

- Do you have regular accountability in your life? Why or why not?

- What are the last five spiritual growth books you've read?

- What is your favorite book in the Bible and why?

- Who is your spiritual hero and why?

Appendix B

QUESTIONS TO ASK EACH OTHER

- What is your testimony?

- What is your ideal church to attend?

- What is your understanding of biblical womanhood? Use Scripture to make your point.

- What is your understanding of biblical manhood? Use Scripture to make your point.

- Do you have any interest in volunteering in ministry? If so, doing what specifically?

- How important is entertainment in your life (e.g., movies, TV, video games, social media, etc.)?

- What are your views on health and exercise?

- What is your perspective on finances and debt?

- What kind of legacy do you want to leave?

QUESTIONS TO ASK THOSE WHO KNOW HIM WELL

- Is he a man worth getting to know?

- What cautions or red flags do I need to know about him?

- What is his reputation like?

- Can you see the two of us making a great marriage?

- Would you encourage your daughter to get to know him?

QUESTIONS YOU NEED TO FIGURE OUT

- Why do I like him?

- Does he push me closer to Christ?

- How does he treat/talk about his mom?

- How does he treat/talk about his dad?

- How does he show love to those closest to him?

- Is now a good time for us to pursue a relationship?

- What gets me most excited about this person?

- What do his priorities reveal about his character?

- Is he secure in Christ or does he "need" me to be happy?

- Have I spent a sufficient amount of time praying about him?

- What do the people closest to me think about this relationship?

- What cautions do my parents/mentors have?

- What cautions or red flags do I have?

Notes

Chapter 2 Seeing through the Fairy Tale Facade

1. American Psychological Association, "Marriage and Divorce," accessed July 29, 2017, http://www.apa.org/topics/divorce/.

2. Steve Doughty, "Celebrity Marriages Are Twice As Likely to End in Divorce: Half of Famous Couples Who Married between 2000 and 2010 Had Split Up by 2014," *Daily Mail*, January 4, 2016, http://www.dailymail.co.uk/news/article -3383198/Celebrity-marriages-twice-likely-end-divorce-Half-famous-couples -married-2000-2010-split-2014.html#ixzz4ZCRW0J6m.

3. Brian Beltz, "Why is the Celebrity Divorce Rate So High?—Divorce Help," DivorceHelp360.com, accessed July 29, 2017, http://divorcehelp360.com/why-is -the-celebrity-divorce-rate-so-high/.

4. "Celebrity Marriages Are Twice As Likely to End in Divorce," *Daily Mail*.

Chapter 3 The Merry-Go-Round Method for Modern Relationships

1. Gary Thomas, *The Sacred Search* (Colorado Springs: David C Cook, 2013), 30–31.

2. Susan Heitler, PhD, "The Deceptive Power of Love's First Moments," *Psychology Today*, July 13, 2012, https://www.psychologytoday.com/blog/resolution -not-conflict/201207/the-deceptive-power-loves-first-moments.

Chapter 5 Getting to the Heart of Love, Marriage, and Sex

1. Joshua Harris, *I Kissed Dating Goodbye* (Colorado Springs: Multnomah, 2000), 67.

2. Timothy Keller, *The Meaning of Marriage* (New York: Penguin, 2011), 83.

3. John Piper, "'May I Have Two Wives?' Six Vetoes," Desiring God, May 17, 2016, http://www.desiringgod.org/interviews/may-i-have-two-wives-six-vetoes.

4. Keller, *Meaning of Marriage*, 42.

5. Thomas, *Sacred Search*, 221.

6. Albert Mohler, "The Bible on Sex—The Way to Happiness and Holiness," AlbertMohler.com, March 25, 2004, http://www.albertmohler.com/2004/03/25/the-bible-on-sex-the-way-to-happiness-and-holiness/.

7. Julie Slattery, *Sex and the Single Girl* (Chicago: Moody, 2016), 19.

8. Keller, *Meaning of Marriage*, 254.

9. Jennifer Strickland, "How Writing a Book about Sex Taught Me the Secret to Love," GirlDefined, August 15, 2016, https://www.girldefined.com/writing-book-sex-taught-secret-love.

10. Keller, *Meaning of Marriage*, 257.

11. Keller, 260.

12. Keller, 259.

13. Keller, 259.

Chapter 6 Taking Femininity into Your Love Life

1. Mary A. Kassian and Nancy Leigh DeMoss, *True Woman 101: Divine Design* (Chicago: Moody, 2012), 27.

2. Kristen Clark and Bethany Baird, *Girl Defined: God's Radical Design for Beauty, Femininity, and Identity* (Grand Rapids: Baker Books, 2016), 136.

3. Elisabeth Elliot, *Passion and Purity* (Grand Rapids: Revell, 1984), 110.

Chapter 7 God's Timeless Method for Lasting Relationships

1. "Psalm 118:8," Bible Hub Lexicon, accessed July 31, 2017, http://biblehub.com/lexicon/psalms/118-8.htm.

Chapter 8 When Your Heart's Desire Is Unfulfilled

1. Nancy DeMoss Wolgemuth, "Betty Scott Stam: A Life of Surrender," *True Woman* (blog), accessed September 14, 2017, https://www.reviveourhearts.com/true-woman/blog/betty-scott-stam-life-surrender/.

Chapter 9 Five Strategies for Thriving as a Single Girl

1. Clark and Baird, *Girl Defined*, 193.

Chapter 10 How to Be "Just Friends" with Guys

1. Harris, *I Kissed Dating Goodbye*, 131.

Chapter 11 Is It Okay to Date a Non-Christian?

1. John Piper, "What Can I Say to My Christian Friend Who Just Got Engaged to a Non-Christian?," Desiring God, December 31, 2008, http://www.desiringgod.org/interviews/what-can-i-say-to-my-christian-friend-who-just-got-engaged-to-a-non-christian.

2. "Is it OK for a Christian to date a nonbeliever for practice?," *Boundless*, June 11, 2012, http://www.boundless.org/advice/2012/is-it-ok-for-a-christian-to -date-a-nonbeliever-for-practice.

3. To dig deeper into this important topic, we highly recommend grabbing a copy of Nancy Kennedy's book *When He Doesn't Believe: Help and Encouragement for Women Who Feel Alone in Their Faith* (Colorado Springs: Waterbrook, 2001).

Chapter 12 Qualities to Look For in a Future Husband

1. Thomas, *Sacred Search*, 45.

Chapter 13 What to Do When He Comes Calling

1. Thomas, *Sacred Search*, 27.
2. Thomas, 26.

Chapter 14 Romance without Regrets

1. Juli Slattery, "5 Lies That Make Sexual Purity More Difficult," *Boundless*, May 26, 2014, http://www.boundless.org/relationships/2014/5-lies-that-make -sexual-purity-more-difficult.
2. Thomas, *Sacred Search*, 211.
3. Thomas, 48.
4. Sean Perron and Spencer Harmon, *Letters to a Romantic: On Dating* (Phillipsburg, NJ: P&R Publishing, 2017), 32.
5. Timothy Keller, "Blemishes in Christian Character, Part 3: Change and Grace," *Timothy Keller* (blog), June 10, 2013, http://www.timothykeller.com/blog /2013/6/10/blemishes-in-christian-character-part-3-change-and-grace?rq=purity.
6. Elliot, *Passion and Purity*, 28.
7. Heath Lambert, *Finally Free: Fighting for Purity with the Power of Grace* (Grand Rapids: Zondervan, 2013), 55–56.

Chapter 16 How Do I Know if He's "the One"?

1. Thomas, *Sacred Search*, 56.
2. Thomas, 55.
3. John Piper, *This Momentary Marriage* (Wheaton, IL: Crossway, 2009), 44.

Chapter 17 What Married Women Want You to Know

1. Elisabeth Elliot, *Loneliness: It Can Be a Wilderness. It Can Be a Pathway to God.* (Nashville: Thomas Nelson, 1988), 73.

"CREATE IN ME A PURE HEART, O GOD, AND RENEW A STEADFAST SPIRIT WITHIN ME."

—PSALM 51:10

"FINALLY, BROTHERS, WHATEVER IS TRUE, WHATEVER IS HONORABLE, WHATEVER IS JUST, WHATEVER IS PURE, WHATEVER IS LOVELY, WHATEVER IS COMMENDABLE, IF THERE IS ANY EXCELLENCE, IF THERE IS ANYTHING WORTHY OF PRAISE, THINK ABOUT THESE THINGS."

—PHILIPPIANS 4:8

"BUT PUT ON THE LORD JESUS CHRIST, AND MAKE NO PROVISION FOR THE FLESH, TO GRATIFY ITS DESIRES."

—ROMANS 13:14

"FOR THIS IS THE WILL OF GOD, YOUR SANCTIFICATION: THAT YOU ABSTAIN FROM SEXUAL IMMORALITY; THAT EACH ONE OF YOU KNOW HOW TO CONTROL HIS OWN BODY IN HOLINESS AND HONOR, NOT IN THE PASSION OF LUST LIKE THE GENTILES WHO DO NOT KNOW GOD."

—1 THESSALONIANS 4:3–5

Acknowledgments

The minute we saw the email from Baker Publishing asking us to write a second book (this book), we almost fell off the couch with excitement. Writing one book was always a dream of ours, but we never imagined God would open the door for a second one. And here we are! As always, this project wouldn't have been possible without the amazing people in our lives and the awe-inspiring God we serve. Join us in applauding those who made this book possible.

God . . . thank You for giving us the Bible—our ultimate source of truth, our greatest resource, and the foundation for this book. Thank you for giving us Your Son—our Savior—the reason we have hope, purpose, and joy on this earth.

Dad and Mom . . . our lifelong supporters and biggest fans. Thank you for your continued support, belief, interest, and excitement. Your constant encouragement keeps us going!

Zack . . . our all-around go-to guy. Your willingness to fill so many different roles has blessed our socks off. From late-night edits, to ice-cream runs, to keeping our ministry on track. You've been an adviser, technology expert, and so much more. We are grateful for all your help and support.

Stephen, Ellissa, Timothy, Rebekah, and Suzanna . . . y'all are the bomb.com. If we could do a huge "Double, Double, This, This" to celebrate with you, we would! Thanks for loving us, encouraging us, and filling in for us during this project. Y'all are rock stars!

Michael, Jamie, Hadley, and Willa . . . your constant prayers and encouragement are priceless. We absolutely loved the spontaneous visits to snuggle with Hadley and Willa. It always gave us that extra boost we needed.

Michael, Carole, Jacqueline, Max, Bri, and Caden . . . thanks for always being there for us during this book project. Your prayers, words of encouragement, and overall interest in our book are always such an encouragement to us. Thanks for being our second family!

Yvonne Welch, Barbara Rainey, Kimberly Wagner, and Heidi Baird . . . thank you for being modern-day Titus 2 women to us and the next generation. We are grateful for your words of wisdom and contribution to our book!

Love Defined Prayer Team . . . your prayers were answered, and this book is the proof. We treasure each one of you.

Harvest Bible Chapel elders . . . thank you for reviewing our manuscript and offering us Christ-centered wisdom and input.

Nicci Jordan Hubert . . . you are a fabulous editor. Thank you for sticking with us and pouring your time and energy into our book. Your insights are absolutely priceless. We are grateful for you.

Rebekah Guzman . . . thank you for believing in us again and giving us the opportunity to write another book. We can't thank you enough!

Baker Books . . . your team is incredible. We have truly loved working with every single person at Baker. Thank you for working with us to publish a second book.

Friends who supported us along the way . . . thanks for sticking with us through book number two. Now that it's finished, let's finally grab a cup of coffee.

KRISTEN CLARK is married to her best friend, Zack, and is the cofounder of GirlDefined Ministries. She is passionate about promoting the message of biblical womanhood through blogging, speaking, mentoring young women, and hosting Bible studies in her living room. In the end, she's just a fun-lovin' Texas girl who adores all things outdoors and eats dark chocolate whenever possible.

BETHANY BAIRD is a Texas-born-and-raised girl doing life with her parents and seven siblings. She is the cofounder of GirlDefined Ministries and is passionate about spreading the truth of biblical womanhood through blogging, speaking, and mentoring young women. To her family and close friends, she is simply a tall blonde girl who loves hosting game nights, is obsessed with smoothie bowls, drinks way too much coffee, and can't get enough of her little fluffy dog.

Continue learning about
God's *incredible design*
for women...

GIRLDEFINED.COM

Girl Defined · · · · · · · · · · @Girl_Defined
@GirlDefined · · · · · · · · · · Girl Defined
@GirlDefined · · · · · · · · · · contact@girldefined.com

SPEAKING
& EVENTS

Kristen and Bethany don't miss a beat when it comes
to sharing God's truth with girls and women of all ages.
The energy and enthusiasm they bring will keep your
audience on the edge of their seats. If the attendees
aren't laughing or crying, they are scrambling to take
notes during these fast-paced sessions. Whether it's a
retreat, Bible study series, conference, or just a one-
time session, your audience will leave with a renewed
passion for God's beautiful design for womanhood.

To learn more, visit
GirlDefined.com/speaking
or GirlDefined.com/events